The Small Business Marketing Survival Guide:
How to Gain New Customers
Without Spending a Fortune

The Small Business Marketing Survival Guide:

How to Gain New Customers
Without Spending a Fortune

By Justin Bicket

THE SMALL BUSINESS MARKETING SURVIVAL GUIDE

ISBN-10: 0990318362

ISBN-13: 978-0-9903183-6-1

The Small Business Marketing Survival Guide:

How to Gain New Customers Without Spending a Fortune

By: Justin Bicket

"Marketing is the black hole of a business."

-Daymond John,
'Shark Tank' investor, fashion & branding mogul

Acknowledgements

First and foremost, I would like to thank God for blessing me with the insight and knowledge that allowed me to write this book.

I would like to thank my mother and father for being inspirations, always encouraging me, and for flat out believing in me.

I would like to express my sincerest appreciation to Mary Ficenec for being there when I needed her most. You have been my crutch...

I would also like to thank Nick H., Patti H., and especially Katie H. for all your help in the beginning. I am truly appreciative for all your assistance in helping me transform my dream into reality. I know I have made many mistakes along the way...

I owe gratitude to my good friend and mentor, Kevin Simmonds. A lot of what I have learned about marketing and business in general stemmed from our late night chats. You helped get me started in the right direction. I am not sure you know how much I have valued your advice...

And to my friends and research buddies Krystall Rae, Trisha Galley, Kimmy Martens and Jolene LaBonte-Eastman. Thanks for all your support and assistance...

I would also like to thank my editor and personal friend Kevin Williams. I would be lost without you buddy…

Last, but definitely not least, to my little angels: Karra and Kyra. You have been my motivation and inspiration in everything I do. I love both of you girls with all my heart.

Preface

(One actually worth reading)

This is a book on how to effectively market your small business, on a small budget. The operative word is "effectively". Anyone can market on a small budget, however, I will show you how to compete with the big dogs, without spending big money. Most small businesses don't have large marketing budgets like the big companies do. This doesn't mean you need to bow down and settle for their scraps. This simply means you have to be smarter about how you spend your advertising dollars, in order to compete.

I wrote this book because owning a small business is a challenge in and of itself. Creating a steady stream of customers coming through your door is an entirely different animal. A marketing strategy is one of the most valuable components of a well-developed business plan. You can have the best restaurant, store, product, etc..., BUT if nobody knows about it, it won't do you any good. I learned this lesson the hard way, and I hope to teach you these lessons throughout this book, saving you some time and money.

I opened my first retail business on a shoestring budget. After opening my doors, I realized I had no (realistic) idea of how I was going to obtain a steady stream of new customers. In all respects I should have failed. But I improvised, fought through, and turned my business into a successful venture. This business is still open and thriving to this day-even though I sold it years ago.

When you open a new business, you will be bombarded by different marketing reps who will attempt to convince you their marketing avenue is the best for your particular business. Remember, these reps work on a commission.

If you listened to all of these reps, you could easily spend over $100K on different marketing gimmicks that may, or may not, work. One thing that is for sure, though, is the rep that got you to sign the contract will get paid their commission.

I was fed up with these reps trying to tell me what they thought I wanted to hear. Early on, I had fallen for some of these gimmicks with their promises of a great return on my investment. Thousands of dollars later, I realized they were costing me a lot more than they were bringing in.

So, I started networking with several other small business owners who had been in business for several years. I started to learn a lot about small business marketing. Remember, most small businesses fail. Any small business that stays open for more than five years is beating the odds. A lot can be learned from these small businesses. Many of them employ marketing avenues and ploys that many other people never think of. By picking the brains of these successful entrepreneurs, one can learn a lot. This is how I became so innovative with my marketing efforts. It's not that I had this sudden epiphany and all things marketing were revealed to me. It was merely a culmination of trial and error, networking, and in the end, just some good, old-fashioned common sense. (It also didn't hurt that I have several personal friends who are sales reps for different media outlets.)

One advertising company in particular that I had issues with, was well-known by several of these business owners. Every last one of them told me they wished I had spoken with them prior to being suckered into signing a contract with this company. They had numerous horror stories of their own about this same company! If only I would have asked around BEFORE signing that contract...

This book exists to educate you about the things I wish I had known prior to opening my doors. I will use HELPFUL HINTS and TRUE STORIES throughout this book as teaching aids. I find that people learn more effectively if a concept is explained first, and then used in a real-life example. This allows them to see it working in the real world, not just on paper. It's not very hard to write something that sounds good on paper. What I show you, I actually use, and it really works.

Having said that, not all marketing mediums are bad ideas for all businesses. Some ideas work better for different businesses in different industries than they do for others. Some of this insight will be included in this book. My business' success is truly attributable to the information contained in this book. When you have overhead expenses, and don't have enough people coming in and spending money to cover these expenses, you have a problem. It's a scary feeling. I am sure many of you have experienced this same dreaded feeling. One thing I discovered years ago is that you can plan for many things in business except for how many people are going to come through your door and spend money with you. Sales projections for a new start-up are one thing, but reality is another.

This book will outline most of the marketing options available, which ones work, might work, and which ones are an absolute waste of money. I will expose flaws in each mainstream advertising medium. I write the complete, unbiased truth regarding these mediums. I cannot possibly give you the correct solution for every marketing scenario, but if you utilize the underlying principles I teach you, then you should be educated enough to find these solutions yourself. I hope you find the wealth of information in this book to be as helpful as I would have.

On a final note; I had no goal in mind for a certain page count for this book. I told myself I was going to write until I ran out of material. I vowed not to go back and add repetitive or unnecessary material in order to boost my page count, as many other writers do. I value your time more than that. Entrepreneurs, like us, do not have the time to sit down and read 400 pages of material, especially when it could have been reduced to 180-200 pages without losing any pertinent content.

This is one of the major benefits of writing from the perspective of an entrepreneur as opposed to the perspective of a marketing professional. Marketing guys will talk your ear off. I understand the importance of your time because I understand the importance of my own time. I wrote this book with what little spare time I had. I made one round of revisions, then sent it off to a professional editor. Their instructions were that they could change anything grammatical, but could not change the content. I have included everything that I wanted. Enjoy.

Author's Note

Anyone interested in opening their own small business or micro-business (5 employees or less), should benefit greatly from reading this book. I write from firsthand knowledge. I, too, am a small business owner. I did not write this book in hopes of becoming a best-selling author, or even to gain popularity as an author. So let me set the record straight: I am not an author. I am an entrepreneur like you.

Being a small business owner means we have a lot of different hats to wear. At the end of the day, we are accountants, marketers, office managers, technicians, janitors, secretaries, graphic designers, etc... Too many businesses fail in their first year or two simply because their owners have trouble mastering (or properly outsourcing) at least one of these positions. I wrote this book to help you understand, and excel in, the marketing department.

Back when I was in college, I took a handful of basic marketing classes. That was the extent of my formal marketing education. I do not believe I started down my entrepreneurial path with much more marketing knowledge than the next guy. Perhaps I had even less than most. It was something that just came naturally for me. Some people are good with numbers, and make great accountants. I suck at accounting, but I have a knack for drumming up interest in a business, product or service.

Most people assume all marketing costs money. This is simply not true. I see it differently. I ask myself this question: "How do I get my message to my prospects in a way that will not easily be drowned out, or ignored?". This is the million-dollar question. The underlying principles behind this concept are what I hope to teach you throughout this book. The bottom line is you do not need to spend a lot of money to effectively market your business.

Contents

PART I: THE CONCEPTS

"People love to buy, but hate to be sold to."

-Anonymous

Filling a Void

Several books have been written with the intention of assisting entrepreneurs in making wise decisions regarding the marketing of their small business. I ran across many of these books when I opened my first business. Most of these books were informative, however they left many questions unanswered. They did not quite live up to their promises. Many of these books did not come from an entrepreneur's point of view. Many of them were written by marketing professionals.

One of the most popular series regarding small business marketing is the "Guerilla Marketing" series by Jay Conrad Levinson. Levinson has written so many books on this topic that the books tend to run together and be very re-petitive. Don't get me wrong, I have the utmost respect for Levinson as he was one of the pioneers in writing books dedicated to small business marketing. However, all the books in this series tend to be a bit long in the tooth and seem to be iterations of the original "Guerilla Marketing" book. They all tend to overlap a lot. It seems that Levinson hit a home run with the original, he and has been recycling the same concepts over and over ever since.

Another issue I had with "Guerilla Marketing" is that it is a bit dated. The original version was published in 1984, and there have been many 'updated versions' since then. However, revisions can only take the book so far. At some point you must realize that technology, marketing mediums, and the world in general, have changed a hundred times over, since 1984. This book could use an entire rewrite, done from scratch.

I would like to note that I am not intending to knock Levinson's series. I am simply giving you an honest opinion from one entrepreneur to another. On the contrary, I believe every business owner and entrepreneur should own a copy of "Guerilla Marketing". My book is great on its own, but it also picks up where Levinson's book leaves off, fills in the gaps in content, and expands on key details. Levinson does have a few good books that focus on specific marketing niches. These are not as repetitive. Examples of these are "Guerilla Publicity" and "Guerilla Marketing on the Internet".

Levinson also writes his books from the perspective of a marketing professional. This is because he is a marketing professional. You have to keep in mind that most marketing professionals have either worked for or owned their own agencies that marketed for multi-million dollar companies. These companies have an entirely different marketing plan, strategy, and overall approach than a small business does, not to mention the difference in budget.

Once again, don't get me wrong, this is a great standpoint for you, as an entrepreneur, to consider. However, I believe having an entrepreneur's perspective is just as valuable, if not more. Who best to show you the ropes than someone who has been in your shoes? Who was an ordinary guy with a dream to open his own business, and actually pursued that dream. A guy who, initially, didn't understand that having an awesome product or service was not enough and that customers don't just flock to your business. A guy that learned the hard way that having a great product is one thing, but informing the public of your business and converting them into paying customers is a whole separate ballgame. This was my experience, and this is the perspective I bring forth in this book.

I am not saying that after reading this book you will know everything there is to know about small business marketing. I am simply sharing the experiences I have had with starting a successful small business and running into challenges on how to get customers through the door. I know what this is like. I have been there. I have also networked with countless small business owners. Throughout this book, I pass on to you all these lessons that were learned the hard way.

NOTES: _____

_____

_____

_____

_____

_____

_____

_____

_____

_____

_____

_____

_____

_____

_____

Justin Bicket

Understanding Demographics

Demographics are simply characteristics of population segments particularly used to identify consumer markets. It's not nearly as complicated as it sounds. In terms of business marketing, it is simply who you want to get your business message across to. Your advertising dollars are precious and limited. You need to devote them to avenues that will show the best (and fastest) rate of return on your investment.

All marketing reps should give you access to their demographics for each of their advertising avenues. At a minimum, they should be able to show you the age and gender breakdown for each advertising medium they offer. However, all this information is useless to you unless you first identify your target demographic audience. In other words, who, exactly, is your typical customer?

For example, I owned and operated a cosmetic teeth whitening retail location. Our target demographic (ideal client) was female. She:

- Was between the ages of 21-55. (Any younger and she probably couldn't afford our services; any older and chances are she didn't have all her natural teeth.)

- Made at least $30K annually, but no more than $125K annually. (Anyone making under $30K probably didn't have the discretionary income to spend on our services; anyone making over $125K would most likely go to their dentist and pay a premium. We were a discount service in comparison to a dental office.)

- Was preferably single. Although we did not hold this as gospel, our reasoning was that single women put more effort into their image than married women.

Although simplified, this is the type of evaluation I hope you have already done. This way you understand who you should be advertising to.

If you are buying an existing business or franchise, these demographics may already be there for you. However, if you are a new start-up, you will need to figure these out on your own. There are many online tools to help you with this especially if your start-up is in an already established industry.

The first step of selecting the appropriate advertising medium is comparing your ideal customer to the demographic audience that particular medium reaches. Common sense is key here. If you sold after-market exhaust systems, you would

Justin's Two-Cents:

"Two good websites for demographic information are:

-U.S. Census Bureau: census.gov
-U.S. Federal Statistics: FedStats.gov"

benefit more from running TV ads during a NASCAR race than a soap opera. This is an obvious example, but I think you get the point.

It is important to remember you can always narrow down your demographic in some way. Many business owners are naive enough to believe that every person is their ideal customer. Falling for this fatal assumption will most likely cause you to take a shotgun approach to your marketing efforts and will probably result in dismal returns. Most start-ups do not have the capital in their budget to waste taking this approach. You need to really think hard about every dollar you invest in marketing especially in the beginning, when, as all us entrepreneurs have learned, every dollar counts.

NOTES: _____

_____

_____

_____

_____

_____

_____

_____

_____

_____

_____

_____

_____

_____

_____

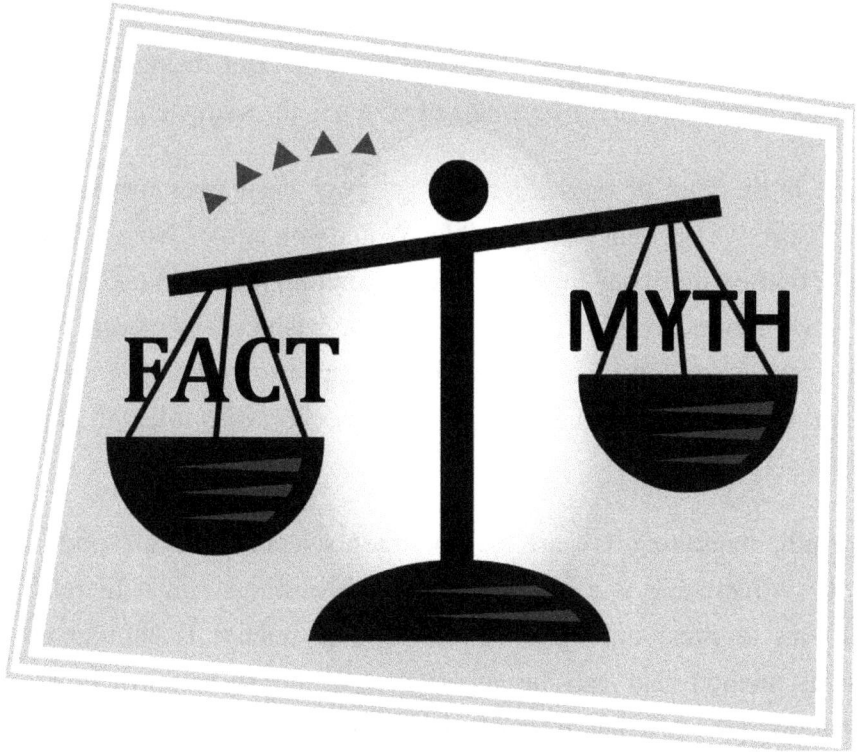

The Truth in Marketing: Dispelling Common Marketing Myths

Many business owners fall for the fatal assumption that marketing is expensive. The naysayers would say that you have to spend money to make money. Unfortunately for them, this is simply not true. Fortunately for you, this book is going to show you how to market your business without spending a small fortune. I'm not talking about surviving or just treading water, but actually being a serious contender without going broke in the process. The vast majority of your competitors have no idea how to market effectively without spending a lot of money.

It's not that these concepts are so profound that I am the first one to think of them. They are actually surprisingly simple. They simply require a certain thought process, a certain attitude. It just so happens that my mind is naturally wired this way. I never actually set out to be a marketing guy. Honestly, the thought of it sounds flat out boring. I am an entrepreneur. I start and build businesses. This is my passion. This is what I do. But, being an entrepreneur requires the wearing of many hats, one of which is the marketer.

What is the goal of marketing? To get your businesses message out to as many prospective customers as possible. Would you agree? Notice that nowhere in that definition did it say anything about spending money. You do not have to spend much money to effectively market your business. However, many small business owners are so unfamiliar with this aspect of running a business, that they end up listening to the advertising reps, because, after all, they're the professionals right?

In truth, marketing is part art and part science. The art portion is the creativity. Advertising is a highly competitive business and it literally takes a piece of art to stand out from the crowd. The science is coming up with a successful method that can be repeated. It's the perfect synchronicity and combination of the two that make a truly effective marketing piece.

One thing that many people (business owners included) do not understand is that effective marketing revolves around perceived value. Notice I did not say actual value, but perceived value. This is the value your customers THINK they are getting. If you take a minute and let that sink in, you will come to see how true this is. You will also see that not even price is as important as perceived value. It is all about perception. In marketing, perception is reality.

Justin's Two-Cents:

"**E**ffective small business marketing is customer-centric, not corporate-centric. Don't focus on your products or services. Focus on what they can do for your customers."

One thing that many small business owners have a hard time dealing with is competition, especially from large retail stores. Every business has competitors. The first thing you need to do is to establish what sets you apart from your competition. I am surprised by how many

Justin's Two-Cents:

"**S**tudies say that your message must penetrate a person's mind nine times before they are ready to make a purchase from you (assuming they have not heard about you before). Further, out of every three times you present your message to them, they only pay attention once."

businesses sole focus is on being cheaper than the competition. They rely on price to be their sole differentiating factor. There are many other aspects in which you can set yourself apart from your competition. These include location, product, selection, promotion, convenience, quality, customer service, and speed. Whichever of these areas you decide to focus on to differentiate your business is your niche. This is your marketing position.

Contrary to popular belief, small businesses (mom & pop stores included) can successfully compete against the big-box stores and large corporate retailers. Instead of ignoring the size difference or always focusing on the negatives of the situation, focus on the positive aspects. (To all you naysayers out there, yes there are many advantages to being a small business.) The many benefits of being a mom & pop shop include:

- having a more personable staff

- honestly caring about each customers experience

- having better quality control

- having better customer service

Embrace these differences. Wal-Mart may be cheaper, but are they as open to suggestion as you are? Is their staff as knowledgeable about all of their products

as your staff is about yours? Will anyone from Wal-Mart mail a customer a thank-you note within 48 hours of purchase asking if they had any questions or concerns regarding their purchase? These are the types of differences you need to focus on in your marketing. Remember, what works for big businesses may not work for your business.

One last piece of advice I have for dealing with the competition is best related using a sports analogy: you can never win if you spend all your time on defense. In sports, defense is preventing the other team from scoring. However, this is only part of the game. The other part is offense. This is where you score your points. Don't just be reactive to your competition. Force your competition to react to you. Be proactive in your marketing efforts.

I want to close this chapter with some words on competitors from Steve Blank, Silicon Valley entrepreneur, author, and business professor: "If you're worried about competitors, you're already out of business. The only people who can put start-ups out of business in the first 18 months are themselves. Competitors really have nothing to do with that."

NOTES: _____

_____

_____

_____

_____

_____

_____

_____

_____

_____

_____

_____

_____

_____

_____

_____

_____

_____

_____

_____

_____

_____

_____

_____

_____

_____

_____

_____

_____

_____

_____

_____

_____

_____

Share-of-Market vs. Share-of-Mind Advertising

There are two categories in which all advertising mediums fall under. First, there is share-of-market advertising. This type of advertising attempts to gain instant sales. It is also the most measurable and, if successful, results in immediate sales. It is usually profitable in the short run. This is, of course, the type of results most entrepreneurs want and expect from their advertising efforts. This is the form of advertising I emphasize the most in this book.

The second form of advertising is share-of-mind advertising. This type of advertising attempts to gain future sales by implanting your businesses message in the minds of potential prospects. It attempts to incrementally increase the recognition your brand has with the people in your marketing area. This is what most entrepreneurs would define as 'branding'. Obviously, this type of advertising is much harder to measure in terms of effectiveness. The results usually take time to see, if ever seen at all. There is just no way to accurately gauge whether these are worthwhile investments for your company or not. Some examples of this type of advertising include radio, billboards and print ads.

Like I mentioned earlier, most of us entrepreneurs want to utilize as many of the share-of-market advertising mediums as possible. Most of us are too worried about our cash flow and being profitable now. This type of advertising is usually easily trackable and, therefore, measurable. We all want immediate results. Share-of-market advertising mediums usually incorporate some type of call to action, whereas share-of-mind advertising mediums typically do not. Some examples of share-of-market advertising can include daily deal sites, Facebook ads, TV segments (not commercials), special events, and even trade shows.

Many advertising mediums can arguably be both share-of-mind, as well as share-of-market. Any particular marketing avenue is not exclusively one or the other. Naturally, there is an element of both in every advertising platform. However, most advertising avenues are going to fall primarily under the umbrella of one of these categories. To determine which umbrella a particular advertising medium falls under, ask yourself if that particular avenue is attempting to immediately convert someone into a customer? Or is it simply just reminding people that your company exists in the marketplace?

For example, say someone is traveling down the interstate. They see your company's billboard or hear your company's radio ad. They could decide, at that point, to go out of their way to stop at your business that day because of that ad. This is not very likely, but it could happen.

However, if someone sees a Groupon promotion you are running until midnight, there is a higher likelihood that they could be reeled in by the Groupon promotion than by the radio or billboard. This is not to say radio and billboards are totally worthless, but they should be used sparingly.

Entrepreneurs should spend the majority of their resources on share-of-market advertising methods. Any share-of-market advertising medium attempts to immediately convert the prospect into a paying customer. However, if it is unsuccessful, the share-of-mind aspect is still there. Expanding on the example given earlier, if Groupon sent an email to 140,000 email addresses promoting your company's deal, chances are only a percentage of them will buy it. Yet, everyone who opened that email now knows your company exists in the marketplace. This is the share-of-mind aspect. The billboard or radio ad transplanted that same share-of-mind without an attempt to gain the immediate sale. Therefore, when you focus your efforts on share-of-market mediums, as a bonus, you still get the share-of-mind advertising. It's the best of both worlds.

This book offers you a great start in the right direction. However, this book is not all-inclusive in regards to advertising avenues. In fact, new advertising methods are created each and every day. The goal of advertising and marketing is simply getting a message through to a large group of people and, hopefully, get some of those people to act.

I challenge you to be creative in thinking of ways to get your message to your potential customer base. Think outside the box. Do not limit yourself to the traditional advertising mediums. I will share many creative things I have come up with, simply by thinking outside the box. Many of these things are very inexpensive, if not free, and often only require your time.

NOTES: _____

_____

_____

_____

_____

_____

_____

_____

_____

Justin Bicket

Tracking Your Advertising Efforts

One of the most important parts of any businesses marketing campaign involves tracking and testing. You need to track and test every advertising medium you use. It makes absolutely no sense to consistently throw money into advertising if you do not know which mediums are worthwhile investments and which ones are a waste of money. There was never a customer that came through my door who was not asked how they had heard about us. Oftentimes, they had heard about us through several mediums, however the one they mentioned was usually the one that sealed the deal.

Testing can be done with any medium. Below are some examples of how some popular mediums can be tested:

- Direct mail/email: you can make five different mailers with different offers and send them to five separate lists of prospects

- Internet Advertising: you can run different ads on Google or Facebook, for example, and their analytics will keep track of how many impressions and clicks each ad has had

- TV Advertising: You can run ads on a couple channels with different offers on each ad or you can run the same ad on different channels with a separate promo code for each channel, if you are trying to get someone to buy online

- Phone Book: If you decide to try the phone book, they can assign you a unique phone number that forwards to your actual business phone number, allowing them to track the exact amount of people who call the number they assign to you

- Radio Advertising: By using unique offers on each station, your customer doesn't have to remember which station they heard your ad on. By mentioning the offer; you will know what station you aired that offer on.

This list is not exhaustive, but by now I think you can see the point. This same concept applies across the board. By tracking your advertising, you learn what works and what doesn't.

Believe it or not, most business owners do not track their advertising efforts. Sure, most will have an idea how good of a response they have received from different mediums, but they have not actually sat down and ran through the numbers. This can be a costly mistake.

A classic example of this is a business owner I know who tried internet advertising for the first time. He got on Facebook and created four different ads and ran a campaign displaying them to his target demographic. Ad #1 never received any clicks. Not a single one. Ads #2 and #3 got a few clicks, but nothing too exciting. Ad #4 did really well. He had a $10 daily budget per ad, and averaged paying $1 per click. By noon every day, ad #4 hit the daily budget max and would not be displayed for the rest of the day. These clicks led to more traffic on his website and eventually to a few more sales. Not an overwhelming boost in sales, but a noticeable and measurable increase.

After a month and a half, this business owner threw in the towel and wrote off internet advertising. He complained that only one of the ads had a good response, and that it was a waste of time. He never did anything about ad #1, or ads #2 and #3. The correct thing to do in this situation would have been to follow these six steps:

1. Study ad #4 to see why it was so successful

2. Study ad #1 to see why it flopped. Ask others for their honest opinion of the ad. Ask them what they like better about ad #4.

3. Delete ad #1 and add the $10 budget from ad #1 onto ad #4 (giving ad #4 a $20 daily budget).

4. Create a new ad in place of ad #1, using the ideas he thought made ad #4 so successful.

5. Tweak ads #2 and #3 with similar changes.

6. Monitor and evaluate what works and what doesn't.

He had the right idea in the beginning, try a few different ads and see which ones catch on. The problem was his

Justin's Two-Cents:

"**O**ne of the biggest mistakes in marketing is expecting instant results, being disappointed, and then changing an otherwise good marketing plan."

response to the information he received. If he would have understood these principles, he would have eventually ended up with four ads that all performed as well as ad #4. After all, wasn't this his goal in the first place? He simply had unrealistic expectations from the outset.

Once again, this example is applicable to any medium. Effective marketing is all about trying something small, testing and tracking its performance, making adjustments to maximize your return on investment, and then scaling your efforts from there.

Instead, he ended up writing off internet advertising as a waste of time and money. This was a terrible error. Please learn from this guys mistake. One of the biggest mistakes in marketing is expecting immediate results, being disappointed, and then abandoning a good plan. This is a prime example of what not to do. Track and test everything. Make sure you ask your customers how they heard about your business. It will pay off in the end.

NOTES: _____

_____

_____

_____

_____

_____

_____

_____

_____

_____

_____

_____

_____

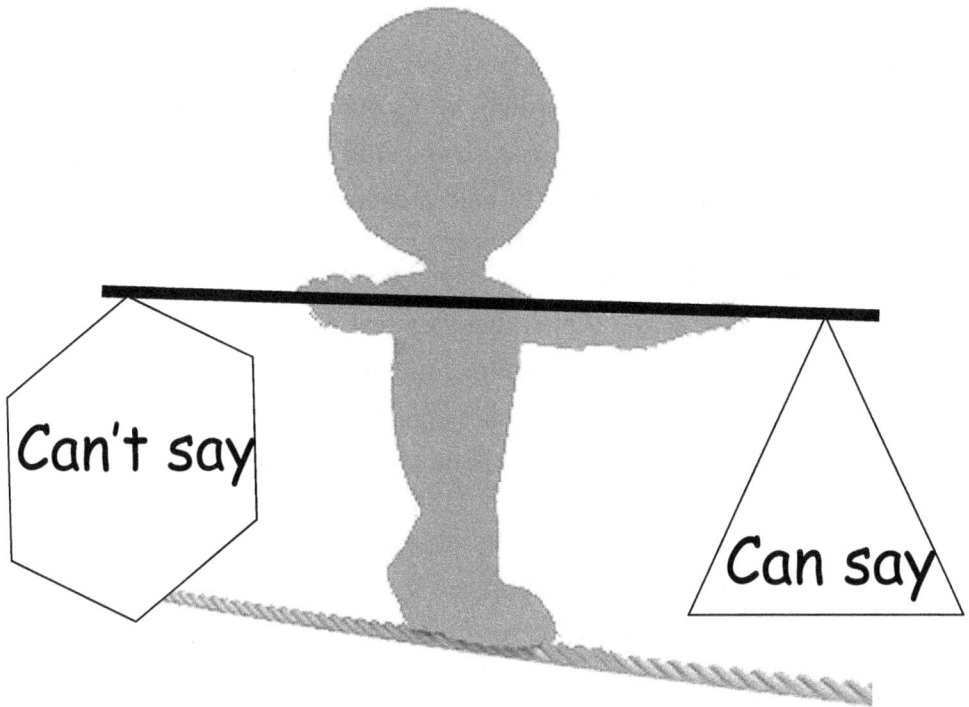

What Can I (legally) Say in an Advertisement?

The Federal Trade Commission's Bureau of Consumer Protection Business Center has some very insightful information on their website regarding advertising claims. I encourage you to visit their website for more info as I will not share everything here. I am simply hoping to give you a general idea of what is OK and what is not, and point you in the right direction. The following statement can be found on their site (www.business.ftc.gov), generally summing up the rule:

"Under the law, claims in advertisements must be truthful, cannot be deceptive or unfair and must be evidence-based. For some specialized products or services, additional rules may apply."

Contrary to popular belief, there is no rule or law against naming a competitor in an ad. There is not even a law against directly comparing your products, services, or prices according to renowned New York advertising attorney Andrew Lustigman. Lustigman works with many startups and has seen many of the common mistakes made by entrepreneurs.

The problems usually arise when new businesses make claims without confirming their truthfulness. "I think there's a real unawareness of the fact that you need to get your ducks in a row before going to market," says Lustigman. "If you're making specific performance claims, you've got to make sure you have tests and studies that are reliable, that back up your claims."

If you are going to say your cleaning product disinfects better, or is greener than that of your competitor, you had better be ready to back up your claims. This is where the tests and studies come into play. There are research labs that specialize in these types of tests and studies. You can find them in your area by Googling "[your city/state] Independent Research Lab".

So who actually governs disputes over advertising? It is a subsection of the Council of Better Business Bureaus, called the National Advertising Division (NAD). They are a self-regulatory entity that rules on competitive advertising challenges. Their goal is to encourage and enforce truth in advertising. Advertisements already get a bad rap with many people claiming they feel ads are misleading. This agency hopes to change that by building "public confidence in the credibility of advertising". Likewise, if you feel you have been slandered or misrepresented in a competitor's ad, skip the threats of a lawsuit and contact the NAD to file a complaint.

Bottom line: be truthful in your advertising efforts AND be ready to back them up, if challenged.

NOTES: _____

_____

_____

_____

_____

_____

_____

_____

_____

_____

_____

_____

_____

_____

_____

_____

_____

_____

_____

_____

_____

_____

_____

_____

_____

_____

_____

_____

Understanding In-House Advertising Agencies

Before I explain this concept, I first need to explain how an advertising agency works and how they get paid. Advertising agencies are companies that a business hires to purchase all their advertising for them. They purchase everything from TV airtime, to blocks of radio spots and programming, to print advertising space. Most micro-businesses don't ever consider messing with an advertising agency.

What most people do not know is that advertising agencies do not usually charge the businesses that they purchase advertising space for. They make their money by receiving a set discounted rate from the different media outlets. They normally receive a 15% discount from any media outlet. Let's say, for example, you are purchasing $1,000 worth of airtime. If you purchased it through the broadcast stations sales rep, you would pay just that, $1,000. If you purchase the same time block through an advertising agency, you will still pay $1,000. However, the agency receives an automatic $150 discount, meaning they are only paying the broadcast company $850. (If you think like I think, you see an opportunity to save $150 here.) This is commonly referred to as an "agency discount".

Now, there is a benefit to purchasing your advertising through an ad agency. You will pay the same exact amount as if you were dealing directly with the broadcasting company, but you will also get the professional assistance the agency provides. This assistance can be very useful depending on the agency you use.

Now let's go back to how we can save this $150 for ourselves. It is actually quite simple. Create an 'in-house advertising agency'. You don't actually need to start a new business. All you have to do is inform the media outlets that you are representing your companies 'internal' or 'in-house agency'. If the name of your business is XYZ Supply, then call the ad agency XYZ Advertising. To pull this off, you will need to create a letterhead for your 'advertising division' (5 minutes on Microsoft Word). You should even print some stationary with the name of your 'advertising division' on it ($15 on VistaPrint or 15 minutes on Microsoft Publisher).

You may also need to have a bank account in the in-house agency's name. This can be done by opening an additional account linked to your regular business account. You may have to use a D.B.A. for this if your business is in the form of a corporation or LLC. This account can just maintain the minimum balance required by the bank and does not ever need to have any activity on it. It simply needs to exist. This can easily be set up in less than an hour.

Once the agency is created on paper, you are ready to go. All you need to do from here is inform the media outlets you plan on advertising with that you represent XYZ Advertising and are interested in purchasing some advertising.

From there you act as the middle man between the agency and your regular business. It's an easy way to save 15% on nearly all your advertising efforts. The one notable exception is newspaper advertising. Most newspapers generally do not give agency discounts.

And yes, this is 100% legal.

NOTES: _____

_____

_____

_____

_____

_____

_____

_____

_____

_____

_____

_____

_____

_____

_____

_____

_____

_____

PART II: THE APPLICATION

"If we could sell our experiences for what they cost,
we'd all be millionaires."

-Oscar Wilde, writer

Phone Book Advertising

Shortly after I opened my business, I had advertising reps from every media outlet calling and scheduling appointments to meet with me. These conversations were all the same. They all wanted to inform me how they could help drive traffic in our door, and how they can do it better, faster and/or cheaper than the next media outlet can. It was quite amusing, yet rather annoying. The most annoying of these reps was a lady from the company that prints and distributes phone books. She informed me of the number of phone books that were printed and distributed and how that would equate to tons of exposure for our company if we signed a contract with them. She was truly relentless.

The one lesson I learned over the years was a simple one: I had to use common sense. Would that particular advertising medium work on me? After all, I am also a consumer. Everyone reading this book is a consumer as well. Obviously there is a little more to it than this, but this is a great question to start with.

If it wouldn't work on you, what makes you think it would work on someone else? This question is not meant to sound as sarcastic as it may have come across. It is actually a serious question: if something would not work on you, under what circumstances could you see it working? I would frequently ask friends of mine, who were women that were in the same target demographic group we advertised to, which advertising methods they believe are most effective. This type of input is often overlooked. Any type of insight that sheds light on how your target demographic decides to buy is invaluable.

I am sure you can see where this is going. I could not remember the last time I had ever used the phone book for anything other than a booster seat for my daughter. Let's face it, phone books are a thing of the past. Google is the most commonly used directory anymore. It has been for a while.

Need to know the location of the nearest Jiffy Lube? Google it. Need the phone number to a local restaurant to make a reservation? Google it. Or better yet, book the reservation using an app, such as OpenTable, from your smartphone or tablet. Bottom line is, with the ubiquity of the internet and Google, as well as a million other online directories, why would I pay to be listed in a book that is only used by a segment of the population that is fifty years old and up? Especially when this is outside of my target demographic range.

The sales rep countered me on this. She told me they had an online version of their directory, and that I could purchase an even more expensive package that would list us online as well as in the print version. They

Justin's Two-Cents:

Here is a story of an actual conversation that was submitted and printed in Reader's Digest:

Needing to look up a phone number at a friend's house, my teenage daughter asked for a phone book. She might as well have asked for a papyrus scroll.

"A phone book?" asked her friend.

"You know," said my daughter. "A book with numbers in it."

"Oh," said her friend as it dawned on her. "You mean a math book."

(Originally submitted by Karen Eccles of California.) *Reprinted with permission from Reader's Digest. Copyright © 2013 by The Reader's Digest Association, Inc.*

had a tiered pricing structure for bronze, silver and gold advertisers. The problem I had with this scenario was that I had never heard of this site. This was a huge red flag to me as I am online everyday and consider myself to be fairly proficient on the internet.

Once again, all roads led back to Google and the other online directories. We were listed on Google Places and several other online directories that were completely free. So why would I pay to be listed on this site that I had never even used, or knew existed? I asked several people I knew if they had ever used the site, I could not find a single person who had. Only a couple had even known there was an online version of the big yellow book.

TRUE STORY

After using common sense in making the determination that the phone book was dated and useless, I inquired with other business owners I networked with about their experiences. Needless to say, they all wish they'd had the same epiphany and not signed contracts with the phone book company. I only found a few that had positive experiences advertising in the phone books. One was an escort company. (Now you know when I say I have networked with all types of business owners, I mean ALL types) The others mostly had an older customer base who probably would never embrace the convenience of newer technologies, such as the internet, anyway. I would like to note that I am not intending to infer that it is a bad thing to have an older customer base. I am simply saying the younger generations are more prone to go online. The older generations tend to be wary of newer technologies.

HELPFUL HINTS

- Make sure your business is listed in as many online directories as possible. Most of these directories will list your business for free. Go to www.submit-it.com to list your website on the popular search engines and directories. You should also list your business on Foursquare, Yelp, and Merchant Circle.

* When you are contemplating advertising on a new medium, remember the best person to play devil's advocate is that medium's competitor. Suppose you are considering spending $300 advertising with ABC Co. Meet with a rep from XYZ Co. (ABC's competitor) and be honest and tell them what you are considering with ABC Co. Then listen to the argument they use to try and convince you it's not a good idea. The rep from ABC will tell you all the pluses. The rep from XYZ will tell you all the negatives. Combine this with the knowledge you learn from networking with existing customers of ABC Co., throw in a little common sense, and you should be able to make a good decision for your business.

NOTES: _____

_____

_____

_____

_____

_____

_____

_____

_____

_____

_____

_____

_____

_____

_____

_____

_____

_____

_____

_____

_____

_____

_____

_____

_____

_____

_____

_____

_____

_____

_____

_____

_____

_____

_____

_____

_____

_____

Radio Advertising

As I stated in the Filling a Void chapter, in preparing to write this book I read "Guerilla Marketing" by Jay Conrad Levinson. Levinson addresses radio advertising in a chapter in his book. Levinson believes that radio is an extremely effective advertising medium. I have to admit there are several philosophies that Levinson and I share, however, this is not one of them. I am not a fan of radio advertising, and would challenge Levinson as to its effectiveness for the average small business in today's world.

This is a prime example of how the age of the original version of "Guerilla Marketing" starts to show. Back when it was written, CD players were a wave of the future. There is even a reference to the 'new' car phones. So many cars are now outfitted with everything from commercial-free, satellite radio to MP3 player docks. The idea of advertising to the rush hour traffic crowd is not nearly as effective now as it would have been in the 1980's. It seems that every day someone comes up with a business model that circumvents the traditional radio station, yet delivers the music people want to hear without commercial interruption. The traditional FM radio business model has been disrupted.

Once again, I recommend using your own common sense. Do you think radio advertising has ever worked on you? When is the last time you purchased something because of hearing it advertised on the radio? We have naturally adapted to ignore radio advertisements because they are everywhere and rather annoying. Not to mention, fewer people everyday are listening to the radio as other music-listening options become available. Many of these other options are commercial-free and play custom song lists, or artists of one's preference, such as Pandora. The radio is being phased out in the same way the internet is affecting the phone book.

For the average small business, the only way I could recommend using radio advertising, is in the event of a big sale or promotion. Even then I would be cautious. I have run across far more business owners who feel they have been burned by radio, than those who feel it was a worthwhile investment.

I would like to point out that it is common for people to misuse an advertising medium, and then claim the advertising medium did not work. Throughout this book, when I use examples of other business owners, I am referring to the group that is actually marketing savvy (unless I state otherwise). I have come across both groups. However, using examples of business owners who did not know what they were doing, and used ineffective ads that were doomed from the outset, would be pointless and misleading.

If you do decide to advertise on the radio, you need to understand the difference between foreground and background stations and programs. Foreground stations are stations which are dedicated to news, sports, talk shows, etc... These are stations that people usually pay attention to while they are on. They are generally not music stations.

Music stations, on the other hand, are generally more inclined to be background stations. They are often played in the background. Think of a lobby or an elevator. News and talk radio would be too distracting to play in the background.

There are instances where music stations can be foreground, such as during the morning radio shows. These types of shows tend to have a fairly loyal listener base. If you really want to use radio for advertising a big promotion or event, I would recommend running your ads during one of these morning talk shows. These loyal listeners are usually tuned in and feel a connection with the radio personalities hosting these shows.

Radio may be good for branding, but usually is not going to translate into instant sales. The obvious, and only, catch to this is in the event of a big promotion or sale. Most of us entrepreneurs have limited capital available for marketing. If this is your situation, your marketing dollars are better spent elsewhere; perhaps investing them in an advertising medium that is gaining in popularity, not dwindling.

> **Justin's Two-Cents:**
>
> "**R**emember, when you pitch to radio shows, you need to pitch a show, and not a story. Unlike journalists, who look for a good story, radio guys are looking for good shows."

There are many things an entrepreneur can do to promote his or her business without spending a dime. They all require your time. If you are not willing to put the necessary time into your business venture to see that it succeeds, then your chances of success are dismal. Most entrepreneurs dedicate countless hours to their businesses, especially in the beginning. However, you can always spend more time, especially if its spent ensuring your business succeeds. Whereas, most of us only have X amount of capital, and, oftentimes, capital is harder to come by than time.

TRUE STORY

I had a momentary spark of genius one day and decided that I would email all the radio DJ's and morning talk show personalities of the radio stations whose listener base was similar to our target demographic. The business I had started at this time was a teeth whitening store and clinic. Of course I told them I was a loyal listener and I invited them to come get their teeth whitened, free of charge. I told them up-front there was no catch. I simply told them, if they had a positive experience and good results, I would be appreciative of them mentioning it on

the air.

Radio personalities are usually on the air every weekday, and talking about the stuff regular people, such as their listener base, talk about. They tend to have a good rapport with their listeners. This is because they are trying to relate with the people who listen to them. All I did was give them a topic for conversation (and a free teeth whitening, of course). Had I not made them this offer, chances are they would have frequented some other business in their personal lives and mentioned it on the air anyway giving someone else accidental publicity. Especially if it was either a great experience or a terrible one.

This will be easier to pull off if your business is new. If they are interested in your product, but have a policy against mentioning businesses on the air that are not regular advertisers, then see the HELPFUL HINT below.

HELPFUL HINT

- If you decide to run a radio advertising campaign, it would be best to get a radio personality to try your product or service free of charge. Then buy airtime during their show and request that same personality be the announcer in your ad. Then allow the personality the freedom to improvise during the production of your ad. If the personality had a good experience with your business, this will likely resonate through the ad. The result will be an ad that actually sounds like a sincere recommendation for listeners to try your business. This way you reduce the risk of your ad sounding like just another scripted ad. The personality's enthusiasm will likely show, leaving the listeners with a sincere endorsement of your product.

- When producing your radio ad, the station will let you preview your ad on their expensive sound system. However, to get more of a realistic idea of what your ad will sound like, listen to it on a speaker like the ones factory installed in cars. This is how listeners will be hearing your ad.

NOTES: _____

_____

_____

_____

_____

_____

_____

_____

_____

_____

_____

_____

_____

_____

_____

_____

_____

_____

_____

_____

_____

_____

_____

_____

_____

Justin Bicket

Contests, Raffles and Drawings

You have probably seen this advertising gimmick a time or two. There are several businesses that put up drawing boxes in their stores or in other high traffic areas. Some may even have their boxes in other businesses altogether. To this day, I see 24-Hour Fitness drawing boxes in almost every grocery store I go to.

They usually offer to hold a drawing once a week or so, and claim to give away some cool prize. There is usually no purchase necessary, all one needs to do is write their name, email address, phone number and maybe even physical address on a slip of paper and drop it into the box. Businesses have been using these drawing boxes as a way to capture prospective customer info for years. The only reason companies hold these drawings is to capture leads for free. Believe it or not, several businesses never even give anything away! Disclaimer: I have several friends of mine who have been selected in 24-Hour Fitness drawings, so I am in no way accusing them of running this scam.

I am a big believer in these drawing boxes. However, I have the complete opposite philosophy of most business owners.

I would prefer to give away more prizes than I advertised. If I say I am giving away three gift cards, I usually give away ten. People love to win things. So why not let people get excited about your product or service? Plus, if someone wins something from your business in a drawing, and has an overall good experience with your company, they are likely to tell their friends. These personal testimonies create a great source for referral business. You create walking, talking billboards.

Like I said before, this is a great way to capture prospective customer info. Not just any prospect, but an interested one at that. How do you know they are interested? Because they took the time out of their hectic life to fill out this form, that they probably figured was a long-shot, to try and win one of your products or services. They most likely want to be your customer, they just need a little nudge.

You are not limited to just offering your business' products or services. There are several other businesses, that have the same target audience as you, that would give you gift certificates to their store for the free advertising. They're happy you are even mentioning them. If it's a big enough drawing, you may even be able to get some publicity from one of the major news outlets such as a newspaper or news station looking for a story. If you do talk the media into airing a story about your giveaway, make sure to inform them of the winner after the drawing. It will help them complete their story, and may get you a little more free publicity if they decide to air the results.

> **Justin's Two-Cents:**
>
> "**O**ffer the owner or manager a free product or service in exchange for allowing you to place a drawing box in their location."

The bottom line is drawing boxes can be placed anywhere and can be a great way to passively obtain leads. Just be sure to empty them regularly, enter the contact info into your database, and actually give something away.

TRUE STORY

After seeing 24-Hour Fitness's cardboard drawing boxes all over the city, I bought four of these drawing boxes. The particular ones I purchased were made of Plexiglas® and cost about $15 each from an office supply store. I made different posters to slide into the sign insert for each of the different venues I placed the box at.

In my shopping complex, just around the corner from my store, was a new frozen yogurt shop about ready to have its grand opening. The owner came around the complex and offered the employees of the neighboring stores a chance to try the yogurt free of charge. (This guy was a great marketer.) We got to talking and I asked him if he would mind if I placed one of these boxes in his shop during the week of his grand opening. He thought it would be a great idea and was more than happy to oblige.

Long story short, I placed that box in his yogurt shop and we received a great response from it. He told me I could leave it in his store as long as I wanted. So I offered to give away one free service per week for the winner of the drawing. Second place would win a $50 gift card to my store. (Note: our lowest priced service was $99, so anyone wishing to redeem the gift card would still have to pay at least $49 out of pocket.) I collected the box on Saturdays and would take it back to my store and draw the winner. Then I would draw about ten names and call each of them and tell them they were all second place. This actually blew up in my face when I called a young woman and told her she won second place and she said her friend had just text-messaged her and told her she had won second place too. Oops.

This same guy ended up opening several stores and he agreed to let me put the box in each one of his stores. This was probably the best $15 investment ever. In six months time, we had obtained over 500 leads from the one store alone, not to mention that I brought at least one box with me to every trade show and event I attended and promoted at.

HELPFUL HINTS

- Ask any and all businesses that have the same prospects as you, if you can place one of these boxes in their store. Worst case scenario is they say no.

- Always bring these boxes to trade shows that you exhibit at and hold daily giveaways. Ask the host to announce the drawing during the busiest times of the day. They will likely oblige since they are all for offering their visitors anything free. This will give you a chance to set yourself apart from the other exhibitors.

NOTES: _____

_____

_____

_____

_____

_____

_____

_____

_____

_____

_____

_____

_____

_____

_____

_____

_____

_____

Trade Shows

Trade shows are an awesome way to advertise your businesses product or services directly to potential customers. There are so many niche trade shows that virtually every entrepreneur can find at least a trade show or two in their area, that serves their demographic. Some of the most popular trade shows are home & garden expos, health fairs, bridal shows, and everything else in between. The average price for a promotional booth varies greatly. On average, the price per booth ranges from a couple hundred dollars to upwards of $1500.

Trade shows are a great advertising avenue. You get to be in front of hundreds (if not thousands) of potential customers. It's the next best thing to having them in your store (assuming you have one). It is imperative you set up your booth as professionally as you did your storefront. Your business' professionalism will be judged by the outward appearance of your booth.

You will need a banner with your businesses name, logo, web address and phone number on it, to hang on your booth. Vistaprint® provides quality banners for very reasonable prices. The trade show host will usually provide you with an 8-foot banquet table and two chairs. You will need to bring along as much promotional material as you can. Make sure the promotional items you bring have your businesses contact info on them. This includes brochures, business cards, key chains, etc... Also, bring copies of any and all editorial pieces that have been written on your business. You will have at least thirty seconds of face time with hundreds of potential customers walking past your booth. More than likely, there will be over a hundred other vendors vying for the same people's attention as you. Needless to say, you need to set yourself apart and stand out.

One of the best things you can do is hold a raffle each day you are there. Offer a gift certificate to your store as a prize. I would recommend only offering gift certificates to your business since you are paying for this time with these consumers and you want the spotlight to stay on your business. Holding a raffle allows you to draw attention to your booth and set yourself apart. It also allows you to build a contact list by obtaining names and contact info of hundreds of potential customers who are obviously interested in a product or service you offer. Since they were interested in trying to win a product YOUR business offers, these are hot leads. Finally, when someone wins, you get a new customer who will hopefully be satisfied with your product or service and become a loyal, paying customer in the future.

To get the best deal on a booth at a trade show, you need to understand how they work. The person or company that runs the trade show, rents out the auditorium or hall. Next, they set up a floor plan with as many booths they can comfortably fit in the available space. Then, they rent these booths to local businesses. Finally, they advertise the trade show on radio, TV, newspaper or other media outlets. Their profitability is entirely dependent on how many booths they can set up and sell.

If you are on a tight budget, I would recommend contacting the facilitator of the show and express interest in renting a booth, but balk at the cost. Once they have your contact info and KNOW you are interested, they will keep in contact as the date of the show approaches. They can always find room for you, and they will negotiate a discounted rate with you. As the date of the show nears, the deal will usually get better and better. They may also be open to a business trade with you, so make sure you inquire about this.

TRUE STORY

I was interested in renting a booth at a local bridal show. I contacted the facilitator of the show about three months in advance of the show. She informed me the show was a day and a half long, and she wanted $1200 per booth. I thought this was too high. I told her I would love to rent a booth but I simply couldn't afford it. She hounded me for the next two months trying to haggle out a price I would pay.

After realizing the price for these booths was not set in stone, and seeing how much she wanted us to rent a booth, I put on my negotiating hat. I initially told her that I would be willing to trade gift cards to my business in exchange for a booth. She countered, saying she would take half cash and half gift cards. I told her this was still beyond my budget. As the date of the show approached, she called me back and said if I gave her $230 in cash, $600 in gift cards and agreed to hold a raffle during the show (which I had planned on doing anyway), I could have the booth. I took the deal.

The lady who ran this show was very professional, yet very pushy. She was a hustler. She and I were a lot alike. She ended up sharing some advice with me. She said you can always get a great deal on booths if you do as I did: show interest, but hold out when price is mentioned. She said they never completely sell out and they will always find room for another booth. If the facilitator knows you are interested, but only willing to pay $400, they will wait you out. In the end, you will most likely end up with that booth for $400. After all, it is $400 more than they would have made. The only downside is that you usually won't

Justin's Two-Cents:

Viva Las Vegas

Why not write off your next trip to Sin City? Las Vegas is the largest host of trade shows in North America. Below are some interesting facts about Sin City's trade event scene:

-MAGIC is the largest fashion trade event in North America, and is held twice per year in Las Vegas. Over the past three years, attendance has increased by 14%, and exhibitors have increased by almost 40%.

-The International Consumer Electronics Show (CES) is the world's largest innovation event and is held in Las Vegas. It attracts more than 150,000 attendees from over 170 countries.

-Of the 250 largest trade shows in North America, Las Vegas has hosted the lion's share for 19 consecutive years.

-Las Vegas has over 10 million square feet of meeting and exhibition space. This is the equivalent of 185 football fields.

-During its 2012 trade show, the AAIW, which is the premier trade event for automotive specialty products, featured almost 2,000 new products.

-The National Association of Broadcasters convention is held annually in Las Vegas, and creates over $20 billion in international commerce.

[Source: VegasMeansBusiness.com]

end up with prime placement in the floor plan this way. Booth selection is usually on a first come, first serve basis. The corner booths and other prime locations are the first to go.

HELPFUL HINTS

- Keep in mind, having an available internet connection or having access to an electric outlet is usually a premium service at these shows. They will likely charge you an extra $100 or so for either of these. If you will need to use an electric outlet, request to be placed next to a vendor who also wants to use electricity, and see if you can share the outlet and the cost with them.

- Go to www.TSNN.com to find a directory of over 1,200 different trade shows across the country.

NOTES: _____

_____

_____

_____

_____

_____

_____

_____

_____

_____

_____

_____

_____

_____

_____

_____

_____

Print Advertising

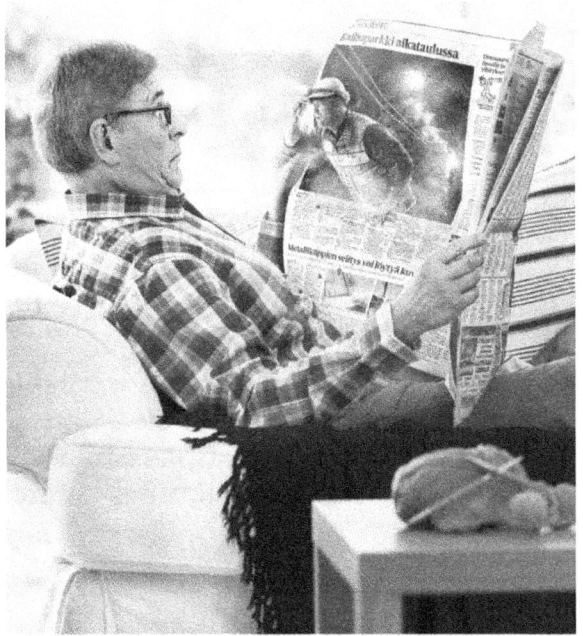

Print ads, such as magazine and newspaper ads, have been around forever. In fact, selling these ads are how the magazine publication companies pay the bills. Print advertising can be very profitable if done properly. However, print advertising can also be one of the worst things you can invest in as well. Many times, the print ad itself is not a worthwhile investment. It is what you do after the ad runs, that is important.

Remember the last time you read one of your favorite magazines? There were probably over 100 advertisements throughout that magazine. I would be willing to bet you can't name five of them. This is because we, as human beings, have learned to skip over ads in search of editorial. We want content, not ads. I am reminded of the quote at the beginning of this book, "People love to buy, but hate to be sold to". We are exposed to thousands of ads and marketing messages all vying for our attention each and every day. So, we have trained our brains to ignore them. It usually takes something drastically out of the ordinary to grab our attention.

However, there are ways you can maximize the benefits of advertising in a well-known magazine or publication. Understand that there are tons of magazines that want your business as an advertiser. I recommend using this leverage in your negotiations. I always look through a magazine in search of articles that are written about (or written by) the owner of one of the businesses that advertise in that magazine.

There are a lot of magazines that will either write an article about one of the businesses that advertises with them, or may even let the business owner write an article, themselves. Editorial articles tend to have a much higher impact with readers than a print ad. It all goes back to the fact that our minds are trained to look for content and skip over ads as soon as our eyes hit the page, (see chapter on "Editorials")

If you plan to advertise in a national publication, make sure you ask about regional editions. Regional editions of magazines have different local advertisers in each geographical area. For example, if you bought a magazine in Phoenix and someone else bought the same magazine in Atlanta, there would be different ads in each magazine if that magazine offered regional advertising. This allows the magazine to sell advertising space to local, small businesses for a much lower rate since the target audience is smaller.

If they did not offer regional advertising, the only companies that could afford to advertise to a national audience would be large companies with huge advertising budgets. For small businesses, this can be great for branding, since your ad may be placed next to an Apple, Rolex, or Microsoft ad. Check the latest edition of "Consumer Magazine and Agri-Media Rates and Data", which lists which magazines offer regional editions and their advertising rates. This is a monthly publication by Standard Rate and Data Service, Inc., and can be found on their website, www.srds.com.

You should also inquire about remnant advertising space with the advertising sales rep of any publication you are considering advertising in. These reps usually have a list of businesses that are interested in purchasing remnant space. Remnant space is the space they have not yet sold when it comes close to publication time. It is the space they need to fill on short notice. Since it is usually whatever space is left over, and usually not the most ideal location, it is usually available for a significant discount. It is not uncommon to find regional, remnant space for over 90% off the national going rate. There is a company called Media Networks, Inc. that specializes in selling remnant space to local businesses in every area. They will provide you with a free media kit if you contact them. Their phone number is 1-800-225-3457.

I would not recommend running print ads in local, lesser known magazines. The reason is print ads, in and of themselves, are pretty worthless. When is the last time you went out and bought something because you

Justin's Two-Cents:

"**A**lways try to talk the publication into writing an editorial or allowing you to write a column or article in exchange for you buying print advertising in their publication."

saw an ad for it in a magazine? Probably never. By themselves, these ads won't bring you immediate business. The reprints are where the value is.

The value comes from advertising in a well-known national magazine and referencing that ad in other media you use to promote your business. For example, let's say you run a full-page ad using regional, remnant space in People or Fortune magazine for $1500. Then mention that you can be seen in the June 2014 edition of that magazine in everything from your email signature, to a framed reprint of the ad in your lobby, to promotional fliers. I would also have a reprint blown up into a poster to use as a promotional tool at trade shows. I would mention this 'As Seen In' claim in every subsequent advertising medium I used.

Justin's Two-Cents:

"**B**lack Friday is the one day that is great to place an ad in a newspaper. It may be expensive, but this is the one day of the year that people buy the paper solely for the ads. Its best to place an ad insert in the paper, and not placing an ad on an existing page though. Also, make sure you run a good special offer, as you will have a lot of competition."

Simply put, you need to milk these ads for every possible value you can. Just running an ad and forgetting about it will likely lead to a dismal rate of return on your investment. It is more effective to run an ad in a well-known national publication. Running an ad in a local magazine does not carry as much weight or recognition. You have to remember that your customer does not know you only ran that ad in your region. They automatically assume if you are advertising in a renowned, national publication that you must be credible. They will think you have paid to run that ad across the entire country. They will also assume you paid an outrageous amount of money for that ad, so you must be a serious, major brand.

Up to this point I have only addressed advertising in magazines and similar publications. Newspapers, on the other hand, are a whole separate animal. I would not recommend advertising in a newspaper unless you are targeting an older audience. Even then, newspapers can be tough because they have such a short shelf life. They are read much faster than a magazine. Magazines are usually distributed monthly, and people spend more time with them on average. Whereas, newspapers are generally printed and distributed daily. Nobody is still reading last Thursday's newspaper. This problem is compounded by the fact that more and more people go online to get their news. It's the older generations, that have read the paper their entire life, who remain loyal readers. Once again, trying to get a newspaper journalist to run a story on your business is a much safer bet.

TRUE STORY

A few years ago I was constantly being hounded by a guy that owned a local coupon magazine. He wanted me to advertise in his publication. It was one of those free publications that were on magazine racks outside of gas stations and grocery stores and just about every large retail chain store. I really did not want to advertise with him but he was relentless.

Whenever I have one of these reps that seems this desperate I consider myself to have the upper hand. I told him that the only way I would advertise with him is if he gave me prime placement on one of the covers (inside or outside), and he would do a business trade with us for the price of the ad. He attempted to counter back asking for half cash and half business trade, but I stood firm.

Justin's Two-Cents:

"**S**hoot for the right hand page for your advertisements. Since people read from left to right, naturally they spend more time looking at right side pages."

In the end I could not get on either the inside or outside cover because he had long-time advertisers that were promised those spots. However, I got the next best thing: a half-page ad on the upper-right page at the centerfold. This is the first page these stapled publications automatically open up to. Plus being on the right side is a bonus. And I got it all for a business trade for services for him and his wife. I didn't spend a dollar. I had a couple people redeem the coupon, but not much other interest than that. During the month our coupon ran, every time I would go to a store that had these coupon books out front, I would open them to the page with our ad and place them back on the display rack with our ad front and center.

HELPFUL HINTS

- If you are going to do any print advertising, look for remnant space in well-known magazines and publications.

- Also look for magazines that have regional editions. If you are patient you can find regional magazines offering remnant space that serves your target demographic. You can gain major credibility this way.

- When you advertise in these major publications, try to shoot for full page ads. They can be fairly pricey, but it beats sharing ad space with several other businesses. At least your ad will be seen.

- Always shoot for the back cover or either inside cover, when available. If the publication is not bound and is stapled, the centerfold is the next best thing.

- Remember, most of the time print ads will not give you a good rate of return by themselves. Use reprints of any full page ads you run in well-known publications. These reprints are where the real value is in print advertising. They are very cheap and can be used forever.

NOTES: _____

_____

_____

_____

_____

_____

_____

_____

_____

_____

_____

Justin Bicket

Editorial

Anyone who has ever opened up the business section of a newspaper or any business journal or magazine has seen stories about new businesses opening in their area. These editorials are great for promoting new businesses. These stories usually highlight the areas in which the business differs from its competition. But most importantly, since they are written with hopes of piquing the interest of their readers, these stories usually make the business seem exciting and intriguing.

Small business owners spend countless advertising dollars attempting to get this same message across to their customer base. So how does one go about having one of these articles written about their business? You have to ask. You need to prepare a press release to be submitted to the many different media outlets. However, just as you customize different ads to reach different segments of your customer base, you need to tailor your story to make it appeal to each individual media outlet you send it to.

When writing your press release, your primary goal should be to turn your message into a great story. Understand, the writers you submit your story to will have one goal in mind: to write a story that will be of greatest interest to their readers. Their sole interest is to elicit a positive response from their readers, so, do the hard work for them. Write an article that makes your business sound like the most interesting, innovative thing since sliced bread.

Now, if the only thing you can come up with to set yourself apart is that your prices are lower than your competitors, you probably need to have someone else write your article for you. There are several freelance writers and services out there that specialize in writing these press releases and articles. You can post your ideas on elance.com, guru.com and scriptlance.com and receive bids from freelance writers willing to write it for you. These services are fairly inexpensive. Remember, these reporters and writers are flooded with tons of these press releases every day, so yours needs to stand out to have a chance of being published. You need to catch their interest immediately. If you do not succeed in grabbing their attention (and keeping it), they will discard your release with all the other uninteresting submissions.

Your release needs to sound like a newsworthy story, not an ad. In fact, it's best to use a real life story. Your story should look more like a narrative, and less like an advertisement. Remember, a story has three parts: a beginning, a middle and an end. Relate to the reader with some type of personal element, then take them on your journey, from beginning to end.

> # Justin's Two-Cents:
>
> "There are subscription-based services that give the names and current contact info of people in the media. Two of these popular services are www.MediaFinder.com and www.MediaListsOnline.com . These online directories tend to be more current than the print versions, since they are updated regularly."

Make it new and up to date. Your story should relate to current events. How does your business solve a problem your customer has right now? If your story makes it past the writer, its next stop is the editor's desk. The two questions any editor is going to ask when deciding whether or not to feature your business, are "Why this?" and "Why now?" Keep this in mind when writing your release. Be proactive by making the answer to these questions clearly visible. Consider

> ## Justin's Two Cents:
>
> **"G**o to the website www.HelpaReporter.com **and sign up to receive inquiries from reporters. If you answer these inquiries, the reporter will write about your business and usually link to your website."**

telling your customer's story. However, if you do, avoid making it sound too good to be true. This is a good way to instantly lose credibility with your audience. Remember, journalists are excellent BS detectors.

Your story also needs to sound unique, even if your business is not very unique. It's all about perception. You need to put a spin on your story that makes it sound unique. Your story needs to stand out from the crowd. Most business owners mass-produce a boilerplate, one-size-fits-all press release and blanket the media with it. This is a big mistake and will make your release look like just another advertisement disguised as a story. This is a good way to get lost in the shuffle.

Press releases are great for grand openings, but should not be limited to them. I have seen several businesses offer a promotional day of free or deeply discounted services simply to attract media attention. Designating a day or week in which your business will donate a portion of sales to charities or cancer society's will likely get your business some good publicity. But only if you alert the media outlets. They can't report what they don't know about. If you can offer the media a sensational and interesting story, they are more likely to feature it.

TRUE STORY

I had several publications solicit me to run print ads in their magazines and newspapers. They would tell me that my business was a good fit with their readership. I am not a fan of print advertising. I told them I had never had any success with print advertising, but I thought their publication was great, and agreed that it probably reached my target audience. (In reality, I couldn't care less about their publication.)

At this point, I went from the solicited, to the solicitor. I told them that since they thought my business was "a great concept" and would be "a great fit" for their publication, they should run an editorial story about us. If it had a good response, then I would probably advertise with them. For some this worked and I got my story published with no strings attached. For others, they would only publish the story after I signed some type of advertising contract with them. This is called 'ed for ad' in the print world, short for editorial for advertisement.

In these cases, I would try to negotiate the least restrictive advertising contract I could sign in exchange for my story to run. Whenever these stories would run, there would be a noticeable increase in interest in our business for about the next thirty days. However, during the months when the ads ran without an editorial, there would be no noticeable increase in business. These stories are very powerful and viewed much more positively than an ad by the general public. People don't believe ads, but they tend to accept articles as gospel.

Justin's Two-Cents:

"**C**ontact any trade publications in your industry and offer to write a free column for some free publicity."

In one contract I signed, I agreed to run monthly ads for a year. Normally I would not have signed such a long commitment, however, this particular magazine was going to allow me to write a full two-page article to be published, and allow me to change my ad size at any time. I decided to run a 1/3 page ad during the month of December, advertising a holiday special. This is also the same month my article was going to run. For the remaining eleven months of the contract I ran a coupon-size ad in the back of the magazine that was only about

1" by 2". The price of this ad was $30/month. The goal was to get my story published. I could really care less about the ad.

HELPFUL HINTS

- Articles and editorials can be framed in a plaque and hung on the wall at your business for your customers to see. They can also be used as props at a trade show, as inserts in direct-mailers, or a variety of other ways.

> **Justin's Two-Cents:**
>
> "**D**on't just think print. You can write articles for online publication also. There are websites, such as www.ArticleSubmitterPro.com that have software programs that allow you to submit your article to a number of directories at once."

You can usually buy reprints in bulk from the publisher for a fraction of a penny each. These reprints are extremely valuable if used correctly.

- Don't just randomly pitch your story to editors. Find a story that has been written that is similar to what you want. Then contact the writer who wrote the story and praise them for a well-written piece. Then try to relate your story to their style. It helps your chances if they know you took the time to read their work and contact them individually, as opposed to just being the recipient of a mass-emailing.

- Suggest external sources of information that will assist a writer in picturing how they could form your story. Try to use independent analysts or other experts.

- Most major publications release their editorial calendars on their website. Stay posted on the features they have coming up and customize your pitch accordingly. Remember, many of these publications have long lead times, meaning they put together a story 2-3 months in advance.

- Writing an article or having an article written about you and your business automatically qualifies you as an expert in your field (at least in your prospect's eyes).

- Here are a few of the more popular websites that publish articles:

  EzineArticles.com

  GoArticles.com

  ArticleAlley.com

  IdeaMarketers.com

  uPublish.info, and

  Buzzle.com.

NOTES: _____

_____

_____

_____

_____

_____

_____

_____

_____

_____

_____

Public Bulletin Boards

Another way to get the word out about your business is to place promotional fliers on community bulletin boards around your city. Some popular places to find these bulletin boards are grocery stores, college campuses, community centers and apartment complexes. This is a great way to gain recognition, and cost you absolutely nothing.

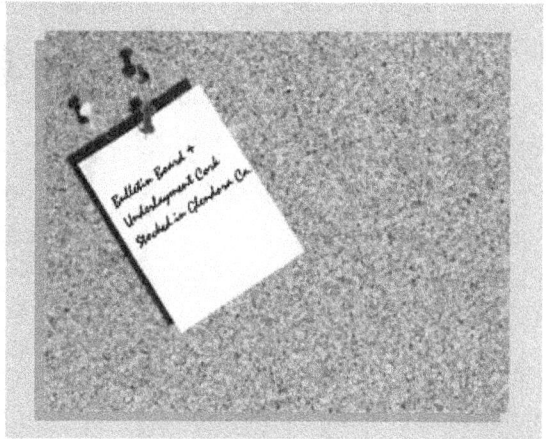

Apartment complexes usually have a community bulletin board located in their clubhouse. It is common to find promotional fliers from neighboring businesses on these boards. Many times they will offer a certain discount to residents of the complex. When you utilize such an inexpensive way to draw customer into your store, you should have the flexibility in your pricing to offer a percentage-based discount, especially since the lead cost you nothing more than the ink for the flier. You should contact the management office of the apartment complexes within a close proximity of your business and request permission to place a flier on their bulletin board.

I recommend taking the same approach to placing fliers on community bulletin boards at local college campuses. These are usually located in high-traffic areas, such as student centers or cafeterias. Once again, I would recommend offering a discount to students who present their student ID at your store. Also, offering a discount betters the chances the powers-that-be will allow you to post your flier.

You may be able to find more of these bulletin boards at local halls, lodges and community centers. All you have to do is ask to place a flier up. The worst thing that can happen is they say no. You have absolutely nothing to lose. More importantly, chances are your competition has overlooked these marketing tactics. Utilizing often overlooked advertising mediums, such as these, is the key to success for small businesses and mom & pop stores.

Justin's Two-Cents:

"**S**ome other ideas of places to find community bulletin boards:
- **Subway stations**
- **Churches**
- **Fraternities & sororities**
- **YMCA's**
- **Laundromats**
- **Malls**
- **Hotel & Motel lobbies**
- **Union halls**
- **Libraries**
- **Banks**
- **Convenience stores**
- **Bowling alleys**
- **Tourist information centers"**

Other often overlooked options are internet bulletin boards. There are many online bulletin boards that are dedicated to different niches. These boards are highly specialized in terms of their readers. Membership to some of these boards are free, but others charge a fee for membership. These bulletin board services allow members to communicate with each other in several ways, including:

- email

- open forum discussions

- links to web pages

- chat rooms

- classified ads

- virtual conferences

> ## Justin's Two Cents:
>
> "**B**oardwatch is a monthly magazine dedicated to internet bulletin boards. It also lists the different online bulletin boards and their focuses."

The primary benefit of using these services is that their users tend to be fairly interactive and want to hear about you. This is assuming you have selected the right forum used by your target audience. If you have done your proper due diligence, the readers of the particular board of interest should be hot prospects. The same rules apply here as to social media: don't just post on the site to sell, at least not obviously. Offer advice and try to establish yourself as the authority in your industry. You will win more customers over this way.

TRUE STORY

I remember that when I was in college, we had a bulletin board located in our student center where students advertised different items. These items varied from cars to laptops with everything in between. This bulletin board also had promotional fliers from several local businesses on it, especially if the businesses offered a student discount.

When I opened my first business, I went back to my school and placed a flier up that I had created on Microsoft Publisher. When I came back a few days later, it was gone. It was at that time that I had noticed all the other promotional fliers had an "APPROVED BY:" stamp in the top corner of each page.

After I inquired with the front desk, I was informed that any fliers had to be approved before they were allowed to be posted. So I asked if they would approve my flier, and mentioned to them that I would be offering the university students a 10% discount. They approved my flier.

Subsequently, I went around to all the other colleges and universities throughout the city and posted similar fliers (after asking permission of course). I did the same at community centers and grocery stores and the like. I received a decent response from these fliers with a nominal investment of time and ink.

HELPFUL HINT

If you wish to place these fliers in a place that targets a certain group of people, it helps to offer them a discount. It will also help you convince the management to allow you to post your flier.

NOTES: _____

_____

_____

_____

_____

_____

_____

_____

_____

_____

_____

_____

_____

_____

_____

_____

Business Partnerships

Partnering with other businesses is a great marketing avenue that is often overlooked. These partnerships can be formed in a variety of ways. These fusion marketing partnerships can include: offering corporate discounts, cross-promotions, business trades and bartering. Creativity is key when coming up with different ways in which you can fusion market with other businesses.

In order for a fusion marketing campaign to be successful, a few key elements need to be present. First, you need to work out a deal with the other businesses that clearly benefits both parties. Second, you need to be able to communicate how this is beneficial to the consumer: How do they benefit from buying whatever deal you are selling? Next, you need to figure out how to communicate this deal to the public: Will you both send out mailings to your mailing lists, or split the cost of a billboard? Lastly, although not set in stone, it is usually best if you and your fusion marketing partner have the same target audience.

Justin's Two-Cents:

"Consider putting together package deals with your fusion marketing partners."

In a previous chapter on trade shows, I discussed how I used bartering to trade gift cards to my store for payment on a promotional booth at a trade show. This is a classic example of business bartering. During the show, the host wanted to raffle off the gift cards I had given her. By doing this, we also received more interest in our booth since they kept mentioning the raffle over the loudspeaker throughout the show. It was truly a win-win situation for our business.

In the last chapter, I briefly explained how to work with management at an apartment complex to advertise on the community bulletin board, usually located in the clubhouse. Another way you can fusion market with these apartment complexes is by designing a flier to be placed in the welcome packets they give to their new residents. You should offer some sort of special deal that is only available to those residents. This creates an opportunity for the management to offer an exclusive deal to their new residents.

To up the ante, gather up about a half-dozen of your fusion marketing partners, and arrange to have each offer individual special promotions, or even package deals. This can be extremely effective since many of your competitors likely have not thought of this. Think about how many apartment complexes are in your city. It is usually best to start with the complexes that are in a three mile radius to your store, and then expand your campaign from there.

Justin's Two-Cents:

"These arrangements are usually a version of "I'll scratch your back if you scratch mine"."

You can also do this same deal with real estate agents. Many of them also offer welcome packets to those who buy new homes from them. In doing this, you receive some passive marketing, and even an implied endorsement from these professionals. The agents receive something of value to offer their clients in return. Once again, a win-win situation.

Another thing I learned is that large companies and corporations like to offer discounts from other businesses to their employees. For them, it is an added benefit of employment—a perk. For the small business owner, this is an awesome opportunity to reach a large pool of potential customers without any up-front capital investment. Usually all this takes is contacting the human resources department of these large companies and inquiring about becoming an affiliate and offering a discount to their employees.

One of the most unique fusion marketing partnerships I have seen was between a large car dealership and a small sporting goods store. These big dealerships have large marketing and advertising budgets. The car business is highly competitive and these dealers are always trying to one-up each other. The deal the sporting goods store made with the dealership was simple: they would offer a free shotgun or rifle to everyone that bought a new truck during a 30-day period from that dealership. In return, the dealership would pay the sporting goods store a significantly-discounted price for each shotgun or rifle they gave away.

Now obviously this was a little more complicated, considering the background checks and legalities involved with selling (or giving away) firearms. However, it was a genius effort and it did really well. The small business really benefited from this by having their name mentioned in all of the dealerships radio, TV and print ads. Most small businesses can not afford to run this much large-scale advertising in such a short period of time on their own. The dealership benefited because they were offering something that no other dealership was offering. Did I mention that this promotion ran about a month before hunting season? It was a brilliant win-win situation.

The number of ways in which businesses can partner up and fusion market together is truly limited by the imaginations of their owners and/or marketing departments. The possibilities are limitless. Generally, there needs to be a clear benefit to both parties involved. Be creative. Use your imagination and ingenuity. Your goal is not to leach off one another, but to find a mutually beneficial deal that helps both parties involved generate revenue.

TRUE STORY

PayPal has a large call center that employs thousands of people, located within a couple miles of my store. I contacted their human resources department and asked them if they had a list of local affiliate businesses that offered discounts to their employees. It turns out they did. The only catch was, in order to be on that list, our business had to offer some sort of discount to their employees. So I offered 10% off to anybody that came in and showed their PayPal employee ID card.

Within the first month we brought in a couple hundred dollars of revenue for an investment of zero dollars. Naturally, I offered this same arrangement to all the other large corporations around the city. Most of them had an employee discount program similar to PayPal's. They usually have an employee's-only company intranet that has a section where they advertise these affiliate businesses to their employees.

HELPFUL HINTS

- The best fusion marketing partners are usually businesses that have the same target customer as you, BUT DO NOT directly compete with you.

- Some of the simple ways you can co-market include putting signs or brochure stands up in each other's store, exchanging web links, passing referrals and/or mentioning one another in your email campaigns.

NOTES: _____

_____

_____

_____

_____

Direct-Mail Advertising

Direct-mail advertising can be a great tool if used effectively. Direct-mail is one of those mediums that often gets a bad rap because it is not used properly. It is also fairly expensive in terms of advertising. One of the primary benefits of direct-mail is that it gets into your prospects home. The hardest part is coming up with a good list of prospects.

The process of selecting which leads to send mailings to is an arduous one. This is the most critical step of any direct-mailing campaign. If you put together a perfect list, but only a mediocre mailer, you could still have a good response rate. However, if your list is too broad and does not hit your target demographic well, it doesn't matter how good your mailer is. I cannot stress enough, the importance of narrowing down this list to the best possible prospects. There are several sources you can obtain leads from in compiling these mailing lists.

One thing I learned the hard way is that you should start compiling your email and direct-mail lists from day one. Every time you obtain a new customer, you need to obtain their contact info. This is important for several reasons. This allows you the ability to contact them to:

- thank them for making a purchase

- inquire about their satisfaction with the product and ask if they have any questions or issues

Justin's Two-Cents:

"**A** great direct-mail strategy can be found in Jay Conrad Levinson's "Guerilla Marketing for Free". Levinson recommends after making a sale:

- Sending a thank-you note to a customer within 48 hours.
- Send another mailer out 30 days after the sale to see if there are any questions or concerns with the purchase.
- Send another note within 90 days, informing them of a new and related product or service offering.
- After six months, inform them of an upcoming sale or promotion.
- After nine months, send a note asking the customer of the names of three people who might be interested in being on your mailing list.
- After one year you send the customer an anniversary card celebrating the one year anniversary of the sale. Possibly including a coupon or special offer.

Each step of the way you solidify the bond with your customer. You do not contact them too often, and your first couple contacts are not sales pitches. This is a great plan for establishing a loyal customer base."

- ask them for referrals

- thank them for sending referrals

- announce new products or services you offer in the future

These are just a few of the possible reasons you need to capture your existing customers contact info. Did you know that studies say it is six times cheaper to market to existing customers than trying to obtain new customers? This is not meant to dissuade you from going after new customers, just a reminder to not forget those who have already made a purchase from you. Every business has one-time customers—customers that make a purchase and never frequent the business again. Did you know that seven out of ten of these customers don't return due to apathy after the sale? These businesses have nobody to blame except themselves for every customer that makes a one-time purchase, only to never return again.

Unfortunately, most businesses ignore customers after they succeed in getting them to make a single purchase from them. This seems extremely foolish, but I have even made this fatal mistake myself. It's not that businesses purposely ignore these customers, it's that most businesses marketing resources are geared towards obtaining new customers. Please remember to continue your relationship with your customers after the sale. Start by instituting a policy that a thank-you note is hand-written and mailed to every new customer from now on.

Another great source of leads for direct-mail marketing is simply using the lists you have compiled from the trade shows you've attended and raffles you have held. These lists are excellent

Justin's Two-Cents:

"**Y**ou can use services like Click2Mail.com to have postcards, fliers, greeting cards and other direct-mailers sent directly to your prospects' door."

because they are full of people who have volunteered their information to you. They most likely offered their info in exchange for a chance to win a product/service, or to obtain more information about your business. Either way, this is a hot lead. This is also an example of how the marketing tactics in this book work cohesively with one another to form one big marketing offensive inexpensively, thus giving you more bang for your buck.

There are also over a hundred different companies that sell leads. These companies have large databases that you enter your 'ideal' customer demographic information into. Then, they will compile a list of names and addresses of a target group that fits your desired demographic profile. However, I would be cautious using this approach. Understand that, oftentimes, this form direct mail has less than a 5% conversion rate. This is because most of the time, these leads are cold leads. This means that for every 100 mailers you send out, 95 will be ignored or thrown out. You may have better results than this, you may have worse results. These numbers are not set in stone, they are simply a guide.

The goal is to come up with a list of prospects without taking this shotgun approach. Even though, technically, you are narrowing down the target demographic, I would argue against the accuracy of any medium with a 95% rate of failure. In previous chapters in this book, I discuss the benefits of holding drawings and raffles. These are excellent opportunities to capture contact info from your prospective customers. Like I have stated previously, these people are already prescreened.

I do believe that direct-mail marketing should be utilized by small businesses. However, this does not mean you should be purchasing these lists from the companies that sell them. The best lists are the ones you create on your own. These are best compiled from both existing customers and prospects who have previously showed interest. Common sense is key here. Direct-mail is not cheap. Postage rates seem to be going up every day. Alternately, email has become an ever more popular option.

After you have compiled a good list, your next step is to decide what type of mailer to send. I personally believe postcards are the best form of direct-mail for most businesses. First, they are cheaper to send. Second, they are automatically going to be read (at least part of them). If you send a mailer contained in an envelope, there will always be some that are thrown out without ever being opened. This is inevitable. Postcards can't help but be read, especially if the offer on your postcard is written clearly and concisely. They do not allow the recipient the luxury of deciding whether or not to open an envelope.

Postcards are also about 60-70% cheaper to print and mail in comparison to a mailer in an envelope. This means, on average, you can send three postcards for every letter/envelope combo. You can also use oversized postcards to stand out.

Justin's Two-Cents:

"**W**rite several drafts of your mailer before finalizing one to send. Once you think you have it perfected, let it sit for a week, then go back and read it with a fresh mind. See if you can make it more clear and concise. Also, have others read it and ask for their input."

Direct-mailers in envelopes can also be effective. Whenever possible, it is best to have the return address hand-written. This adds a personal touch, as it does not look like just another bulk-mailed advertisement. However, this is not always feasible, especially if you are sending a mass-mailing.

To increase your open rate, I would recommend inserting some irregular shaped object inside the envelope. This creates a natural curiosity in people. They want to know what is inside. A very inexpensive option is a balloon that is customized with your business logo and contact info on it. This serves as a promotional tool as well as something to pique the curiosity of your prospects and hopefully increase the open rate of your envelopes.

Justin's Two-Cents:

"**L**eaving the return address blank on the envelope of your direct-mailer creates a natural curiosity and will incline the recipient to open your envelope. It's hard to throw something away when you don't know who it's from."

Justin's Two-Cents:

"**I**f you ever have an editorial piece written about your business, be sure to include a reprint of it in your direct-mailer."

When sending a mailer in an envelope, you need to put a lot of thought into both the mailer and the envelope. The envelope is the creative package containing your great offer. The offer is no good if the package doesn't get opened. Think of the envelope as a book cover. Most people scan the back cover to decide whether to read the book or not. The same principle applies to the envelope of your direct-mailer.

You need to use a teaser of some kind, or wording that entices your prospects to actually open the envelope. Be creative with the envelope. Everything from the color to the wording and even the placement of the wording should be creatively thought out. What would work on you?

Consider including some wording on the backside of the envelope. Many businesses fail to use this space to attract attention to their envelope. You have a 50% chance that when the person picks up the envelope it will be back side up. Take advantage of this. Whatever you do, make sure your envelope will stand out from the rest.

In your sales letter include the special offer in clear and concise wording. Here are a few tips on improving the response rate for your mailers:

- Don't limit yourself to text only. Use graphic illustrations, photos of your product, or anything that will help someone make the decision to buy from you.

- Remember people love ANYTHING that is free.

- Focus on your customer more than your business. You should use the words 'you' and 'your' three times for every occurrence of 'I', 'Me' or

'We' in your sales letter.

- Use vivid language.

- Highlight the important phrases or sentences to make them stand out from the regular text. This will help stress these points to your prospects.

- Your sales letter should CLEARLY explain your offer AND explain what steps your prospects should take next.

- Use a P.S. at the end of your sales letter.

Remember to always ask yourself what works on you. This is universally applicable across any medium. I find that this puts you in a great starting position. What was the last direct-mailer that caught your attention and stood out among the pile of junk mail? What, exactly, made it stand out?

One thing that I believe is important is adding a P.S. at the end of your sales letter. This gives you the chance to restate your offer. Perhaps tweak the wording a bit in case the letter didn't quite seal the

Justin's Two-Cents:

"**S**tart with smaller mailings, test and track your results, then scale from there. Come up with a successful formula that can be scaled and repeated."

deal. I would also recommend to have the P.S. written in a different color and font than the body of the sales letter.

The last thing I will focus on is the offer itself. You do not have to include a special offer for a direct-mailer, but don't expect good results if you do not. Special, limited-time offers create a sense of urgency and encourage your prospects to act swiftly. Remember, you have a lot of junk mail as competition and if they are reading your offer, then you have succeeded in getting the prospect to open the envelope to learn more. Do not let them down at this point. You have worked hard to get them this far. Make sure the offer is worthwhile.

The whole package needs to flow naturally in order for a direct-mail campaign to be effective. The envelope needs to create a sense of excitement or anticipation in the prospect's mind. Once they open it, the sales letters, offer and call to action need to be seamless. There needs to be a natural progression. Don't jump from one idea to the next. A confused prospect will often become a lost prospect. Keep their excitement building until you lay out the call to action. This is where you explain how, exactly, they can take advantage of your offer.

Bottom line is, direct-mail can be effective if your offer is sent to the right audience. If you're on a tight budget, I would recommend only using lists of hot leads. If you cannot afford to lose the money you would spend obtaining a list of cold leads, then do not do it. Instead, focus your direct-mail efforts on the leads you obtain through trade shows, drawings and other ways people have volunteered their contact info to you. Try to personalize these whenever possible. Also, remember to direct-mail your existing and previous customers.

TRUE STORY

I signed up for a direct-mail campaign with a company that mails envelopes full of coupons. Obviously, this approach is not as good as sending out a single mailer, but it is less expensive. I had met with the rep of this company at a health & wellness expo I attended as an exhibitor.

I was able to reach 50,000 homes within certain Zip Codes which I had hand selected. These Zip Codes were physically located in the epicenter of my target market area located around my store. My coupon was slightly smaller than a #10 envelope. All the coupons were the same size in this packet. There were over forty other coupons for various businesses (some of these were direct competitors of mine, which I did not know prior to the mailing). The cost of a four month campaign to mail to 50,000 homes was $1150 per month. Of course they required me to sign a contract. This company all but guaranteed me a 2-3%

conversion rate. This means I would have had 1,000-1,500 new customers as a result of this campaign. It sounded like a really good idea...on paper.

In reality, I only received five leads from this campaign. All of these leads did convert to sales. However, this equates to a .0001% return. This is a far cry from the 2-3% they insinuated I would receive.

After running this campaign for two months, I attempted to cancel our contract. There was wording in the contract that stated I could cancel before a new mailing was sent out. The reps wife ended up telling me that I could not opt out of the contract and that they were sending the ad copies to the printer the next week for the third month of my contract. I told her not to do it because I couldn't afford to throw money away by running these ads. Long story short, they sent out the mailing anyway and then we fought over the contract for several months.

Many of these advertising companies are sleazy. You need to be wary of signing any contracts. Always network with other business owners to find great marketing tips and tools. Networking is also beneficial in researching these advertising companies track record.

I later found several other business owners who said they wished I would have spoken to them before signing that contract. Several of these business owners had horror stories of their own about this same company. After reading some online small business marketing forums, I found several negative reviews from other small business owners regarding the same issues I had with this company.

I would also like to note that I continued to market to this same demographic area that these mailers were being sent to. This area was located in the five Zip Codes surrounding my store and the homeowners there also fit into the income bracket of our 'ideal' customer. Through rigorous tracking, we discovered most of our customers were coming from these five Zip Codes.

This told me that we were hitting the right people, but the bulk coupon-mailing company was a poor medium. I do not recommend using these bulk coupon-mailing companies. Their sole interest is to sign up as many businesses as possible and filling this packet with as many ads as possible. This medium might be more effective if there were a dozen or less advertisers per packet.

My goal with this book is to give you the absolute truth, and in the spirit of objectivity I want to mention an exception I came across. A friend of mine owns a sub-sandwich shop. He uses this same bulk coupon-mailing company and swears that it is his best source of leads. The special offers he usually advertises are along the lines of buy one sandwich, get one free. However, he is the only business owner that I have networked with that had anything positive to say about this particular company. He said that in the end, he pretty much breaks even every month with the business he generates using these mailers. However, I did not call all the advertisers in this packet and ask about their success with this medium. If you are considering a medium like this, perhaps you would be best served by calling some of their existing advertisers and inquire about their success.

HELPFUL HINTS

- Don't think that direct-mailing automatically means mass-mailings. The beauty of direct-mail campaigns is that you can be as broad or narrow with your targeting as you would like. Direct-mailing can be five mailers or 500,000 mailers.

- Statistically, the best months are January, February, and October. The worst time of year for sending direct-mailers is March through June. For business-to-business mailings, try the first three months of the year.

- Understand that people are always moving. If your list is a few years old, it may be stale and out of date. You need to expect about 15% of the addresses on your list to change every year. Email addresses tend to be a bit more permanent. Most people only change emails if their account has been compromised, or if they receive too much 'spam' mail.

- Focus on your customer in your direct-mailer. Many businesses fall into the trap of talking about themselves and how wonderful their product/service is. This actually turns people off. Focus on issues or problems your prospects have and how your product/service can help by serving as a solution that makes their life easier.

- Keep your lists separate. If you have contact info for 150 prospects that you obtained at a bridal show, keep this separate from the list you compiled at a charity fundraiser. This allows you to send specific mailings to the groups that all have something in common. For example, you would want to send a wedding special to those you signed up at a bridal show, but not from the fundraiser.

- Try using black as a primary color in your advertisement, with red as an accent color. Don't overuse the red though. It is a good color to draw attention to something as long as you don't overuse it like most businesses do.

- Look into obtaining mailing lists from home shopping networks. These lists consist of leads that have track records of making purchases direct-marketed to them.

- Check out Direct Marketing Magazine.

NOTES: _____

_____

_____

_____

_____

_____

_____

_____

Justin Bicket

Email

Email can be one of the best marketing tools in a small business' arsenal. However, it is also one of the most abused. This is evidenced by the millions of messages sent each day that are marked as spam. Unfortunately, some seedier businesses and scams have flooded people's inboxes leaving them feeling inundated and weary. However, this merely poses a challenge that an entrepreneur must overcome. Email can still be effective if used properly.

Many of the same principles that apply to direct-mail campaigns also apply to email. Both need to be short, sweet and contain a call to action. Instead of an envelope, you have a subject line. Both of their success rates are primarily dependent upon how accurately their

Justin's Two-Cents:

"**D**id you know that U.S. businesses spend billions of dollars to gain sales leads each year? Did you also know they lose 70% of them due to not making contact quick enough? Dr. James Oldroyd of MIT conducted a study of over 600 companies that found the odds of a lead entering the sales process were 21 times greater if the business made contact within 5 minutes of generating the lead versus contact within 30 minutes."

lists represent their target demographic. Don't get me wrong, the message itself is important, but without a good list, the message has no chance.

In the previous chapter on direct-mail marketing, I focused on how to build the best lists, so I will not go back over that here. The same principles apply to both lists.

Justin's Two-Cents:

"**M**ore emails are opened on Tuesdays and Wednesday than any other day."

Before embarking on an email campaign, you need to need to figure out what, exactly, you hope to accomplish. Meaning, if the campaign is successful, what action would you like your prospective customers to take. Once you know what end result you are seeking, next you need to map out how to get them there. There are three steps that need to be connected seamlessly: Subject line ➡Message ➡Destination

After you have a good list put together, the first step is the subject line. This is arguably the most important step. It is here that you either lose the customer or grab their interest and invite them to learn more. The subject line needs to be concise. Say as much as you can, in as little space as you can. As a general rule of thumb, try to keep your subject line to fifty characters or less. Before ever making it to a human recipient, though, you have to first make it past the spam filter.

The spam filter is what decides what emails are genuine and which ones are shady, mass-mailed messages. Believe it or not, this is an obstacle you should welcome. If it wasn't for spam filters, people would be so overwhelmed with countless emails from shady businesses that a legitimate email wouldn't stand a chance of being read. You need to understand how the spam filters work in order to get around them. The following is a list of a few words and phrases that will most likely trigger the spam filter if used in your subject line or message:

- For pennies a day

- Free gift

- 100% Guaranteed

- Initial Investment

- Money-making

- Take action now

- Double or triple your _____

- Earn thousands from home

These are just a few examples. You can find updated lists online by Googling "spam keywords".

After making it past the spam filter, you now have the human element to deal with. People these days are fairly savvy when it comes to advertising. It usually helps to have the subject line

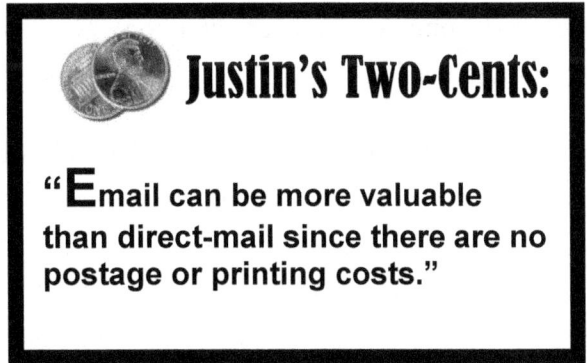

Justin's Two-Cents:

"**E**mail can be more valuable than direct-mail since there are no postage or printing costs."

personalized with their first name. This will help you make it past the spam filter, as well as catch the reader's attention. A few examples of good subject lines that should make it past spam blockers while using the first name in the subject line are:

- Karra, sorry we missed you

- A courtesy reminder for you, Tony

- Kyra, did you remember?

- Tim, did you see this?

- Need your advice, Jeanette

- Felicia, did you forget?

- Print this page, Wayne

- Sopa, the info you requested

- Alex, remember this?

These are just a few examples. Many experts believe the best approach is to clearly state what you are offering in the subject line. Think about how many email messages you have deleted without ever opening, because the subject line did not grab your attention. A good tactic is to go through your inbox and look back as far as the messages are archived and take note of well-written subject lines that commanded your attention. This should give you an idea of what direction to head in.

The next step is your message. The body of your message needs to be short and sweet. As you go through these three steps you are giving a little more information each time. The subject line is the shortest, followed by the message. The message is obviously going to be longer than the subject line, but should still be brief. Remember, people don't have the time to read every email they receive.

If you have succeeded in getting them this far, keep in mind their time is valuable. Get to the point quickly and concisely. A good rule of thumb is to make your entire email readable on one screen without having to scroll down.

Justin's Two-Cents:

"Compose your emails in HTML which allows you to add graphics and add color to make them stand out. Just don't go overboard."

Clearly state the reason for your message (usually a special offer). Then insert a hyperlink to your website. You need to clearly state what you would like them to do next. Do you want them to go to your website to book an appointment, to learn more, or to actually make a purchase? Maybe you want them to print a coupon in the email, then redeem it at your store. Whatever it is you are trying to get them to do, make sure it is clear. If you have brought them this far, they are obviously interested.

The last step is your destination. In the subject line of the email we tried to keep it to fifty characters or less. Then in the message itself we used only what would fit on the computer monitor without requiring them to scroll down. The destination is likely either your website, physical location or maybe a phone call to you. At any of these destinations you have all the time and space you need. This is where they can find out anything and everything else they would like to know. They are visiting your store or website because they want this information. It's all about progression. They simply want to know how, exactly, they will benefit by taking you up on your offer.

Above, we discussed the most popular type of email campaign: the special offer. There are other valuable ways of using email effectively, such as offering a regular newsletter. An effective and popular format of these offers is offering a 'tip of the week'. You can also educate your subscribers in some way, or offer a solution to their problem. The key is to not try to sell them here. This is the share-of-mind approach to email marketing, whereas, the special offer emails are share-of-market. If you want to be successful using email marketing, you would be wise to utilize both of these efforts. By sending out the newsletter, your customers and prospects will soften up to you, after realizing you are not trying to sell them something with every email you send them. The goal is for them to eventually look forward to hearing from you. Then you use special offers sparingly. You can even attach a coupon to your newsletter if you would like.

Many business owners I have networked with love the idea of sending a weekly or monthly newsletter. However, they simply do not have the time to do so. Many of them do not consider the obvious way to solve this problem: outsource it. Jonathan Taylor discusses this option in his book "The Official Small Business Guide to Web Marketing 2.0" Taylor recommends using www.Need-An-Article.net. This is a subscription-based site that charges a nominal monthly fee (around $10/month), and then charges per article. Taylor uses the example of a 550-word article costing $5.50, or about a penny per word. This is extremely affordable for the quality of work you get.

Keep in mind that your prospects and customers that gave you their email address trust you. They trust you to not share it with a third party. More importantly, they trust you to not swamp them with offers. They signed up because they were interested in your business, wanted your expertise, or simply wanted to keep in contact with you. Do not abuse this trust. If you would have told them you were going to bombard them with special offers, how many people would have volunteered their email address? Likewise, if they sign up because you promised them a regular newsletter, make good on that promise. Don't send advertisements that are simply called newsletters. Respect your customer's time and privacy.

TRUE STORY

A friend of mine ran regular soccer camps for kids. Naturally, he had a long contact list of about 400 soccer moms in the area. I was opening my store about a month or two before he was getting married. Over lunch one day, he mentioned that his fiancé wanted them both to get their teeth whitened before the wedding. In the same conversation I mentioned that I was going to start gathering email addresses to build an email database to market to. Long story short, we traded teeth whitening services, for both he and his wife-to-be, in exchange for a copy of his email list.

I thought this would be a great idea. This is before I knew about the opt-in rules with email. I ended up sending out an email blast to this list for a 'soccer mom special'. The response was not what I hoped for. I had replies and calls from recipients who wanted to know how I got their email address. I didn't want to throw my buddy under the bus, so I told them I bought the lists from a lead service.

This was not the appropriate way to go about this. We could have fusion-marketed together. He could have sent out his newsletter mentioning us, and inserted a special offer available only to the parents of kids in their program. Or he could have inserted a hyperlink to our website where people could opt-in to learn more. Bottom line is, there was nothing wrong with the email mentioning us or our promotion, but it should have come from him.

This is a great example of how people expect businesses to respect their privacy when trusting them with their personal information. What do you think would have happened if I would've told the email recipient where I got their email address from? The best lists are the ones built from people who opt-in.

<u>HELPFUL HINTS</u>

- Keep an eye out for good headlines in newspapers. The same principle used in forming good headlines should be used in coming up with a subject line for emails.

- Write your email messages casually as if you are having a personal conversation with the person. This helps you avoid sounding too pitchy.

- HelloWorld.com, ConstantContact.com, Aweber.com and HubSpot are all programs that will automate every bit of your email marketing campaigns. They will do everything from track your open-rates, to personalize the emails, and even auto respond. Many of them have templates that will help you design these emails. These services have come a long way in terms of covering everything to do with email marketing.

Your Website and Online Presence

I hope that your business is far enough into this century that your company has a website. To be considered a serious contender in your industry, you need to have a website and an online presence. There are hundreds of services out there that will allow you to build a website for free, or relatively inexpensively. For this chapter, we will assume you already have a website up and running. We will deal with the issues of generating traffic, increasing interest and just increasing your web presence in general. Remember, there is a lot riding on your website. It is constantly working for, and representing, your business. It must convey professionalism and brand, communicate the proper message, and it must engage its visitors.

Online Directories and Search Engine Listings

One of the first things you should do after launching your website is submit it to the listing directories. This is the first step in getting your site to pop up on search engines when someone searches for products or businesses in your industry. If you do not register with these search engines, they have no idea you exist. It is about as important as being listed in the phone book was thirty years ago. Some of the major search engines and directories you should be registered on are:

- Google.com/addurl

- Yahoo!

- MSN

- Bing

- Yelp

- Foursquare

- Merchant Circle

- CitySearch

- Insider Pages

- BizWeb.com

- Commerce.net

You have to remember that, oftentimes, these sites are the modern day phone book. When people want to locate the nearest sushi restaurant, they will Google it on their smartphone. Not only do they get multiple listings instantly, but they also will see reviews and directions with a couple taps of the touch-screen. If you do not list your business, then it will likely get listed anyway, eventually. However, in these instances it is not uncommon for the listing to have an incorrect address or phone number, which could potentially cost you a lot of business.

Affiliate Programs

If you sell online, you can use online affiliate programs to increase your sales. Customer affiliate programs allow users to promote your products online, and in return, receive a commission off of each sale they make for you. The internet is full of hustlers and salespeople out there who are all about making a buck. A handful of the more popular affiliate programs are:

- ClickBank.com

- Cj.com

- Amazon Associate Program

- LinkShare.com

- PayDotCom.com

- AssociatePrograms.com

- ClickBooth.com

- Commissionsoup.com

Many of these programs are designed for those with online businesses to cross-promote one another's products in related industries. These are usually products that compliment, but do not directly compete with, your current products or services. Obviously it is best if the products appeal to the same target audience. You can either allow another business to place ads and links on your site, or you can advertise your products through their site. You can also find sites that offer affiliate programs by navigating their site and looking for a section titled "Associates" or "Affiliates" in their site map.

You need to choose an affiliate program carefully. If you are not familiar with these programs, you may want to feature others' products on your site before setting up a program to pay affiliate sellers. This will allow you to see how the commission structures are designed, how sales activity is monitored, and how links and unique sales-tracking codes are used. These programs, used effectively, can not only help market your business with no up-front capital requirement, but can also provide an additional source of revenue by listing affiliates on your site as well.

Search Engine Optimization (SEO)

Search engine optimization (SEO) is another concept you need to be familiar with. To understand SEO you must first understand how search engines work. They send out virtual spiders that continuously 'crawl' all over the Web (World Wide Web that is) and search for new websites as well as updates for existing sites. These sites are then gathered, indexed and categorized using complex algorithms that decide which websites are the best and most reliable match for the search criteria entered.

Your websites use of meta-tags plays a large role in this process. (My intention is not to get too in-depth with computer programming in this book since the focus is on marketing. However, I feel it is important to quickly explain this concept.) Meta-tags are specific lines of HTML programming contained in a website which categorize the sites content, accurately. This ensures that when someone searches for something on a search engine, the most relevant hits pop up. If you need assistance creating meta-tags, you can check out one of these links:

- AnyBrowser.com/MetaTagGenerator.html

- iNeedHits.com/free-tools/free-metatags.aspx

SEO is basically trying to optimize your placement on search engine results. Like I stated before, they utilize a complex algorithm which is extremely hard to deceive or manipulate. SEO companies specialize in manipulating your placement with these sites. Some of the things that can be done to increase your ranking include:

- have several reputable sites post links to your site (backlinks)

- choose accurate lists of keywords in your site's programming and when you register your site with the search engines

- increase your traffic: the more popular your site is, the more favorable the search engines tend to treat your site

Justin's Two-Cents:

"**D**o a quick Google search of your business name and make sure that all sites that mention your company also post a link to your website. If you find some that don't, email the owner and request a link to be posted."

One of the options I have listed above is having reputable sites post links to your site on their site, otherwise known as backlinks. Think of this as a recommendation. The search engines view this as a reputable company is placing their stamp of approval on your business. They are doing this objectively and have nothing to gain, so it must be credible.

However, sometimes these links can be hard to obtain. The reason for this is that there is no benefit for a website owner to post a non-reciprocal link to your site. On the other hand, if you both post links to each other's site, it will not have nearly as much benefit when it comes to SEO. The best links are direct, one-way links from other sites to yours.

One of the best tricks to find sites that will be willing to link to your site is by checking out who links to your competitors sites. Sounds complicated, huh? This is actually very simple. You simply go to Google (actually, any search engine will work just fine) and type in the word "link:" before your competitors domain name. So, if your competitors domain name is www.AssetBackers.com, then you would Google "link: AssetBackers.com". Once you hit the search button, a list of websites that link to the www.AssetBackers.com site will populate. Once you

> ### Justin's Two-Cents:
>
> "**V**isit www.SpamHaus.org to check hosting companies' reputations. Some have bad reputations and even get blacklisted for allowing illegal mail campaigns."
>
> **AhRefs.com**
>
> **or MajesticSEO.com"**

have this information, ask those website owners if they would link to your site as well. There is a good chance they will.

Another thing I would like to touch on is increasing traffic to your site. Like I mentioned above, the more traffic you get, the more favorable the search engines will treat you. There are services out there that promise to send you thousands of hits to your site for a fee. One example of this is an ad I saw in the back of a recent business magazine that advertises: "10,000 VISITORS delivered to your website! Only $199. www.TheBestAdvertisingSite.com". I have not used these sites, nor do I know of anyone who has. Therefore, I cannot make any statement as to the validity or effectiveness of these services. I am a bit curious though...

The last point mentioned in the list is selecting proper keywords. Keyword selection can make or break your site. You need to use an appropriate keyword density (generally 2-5%) and placement (it is generally the best to list keywords as the last words on a webpage). It is also best to avoid being overly generic in your keyword selection. If you have a website that is dedicated to German Shepherds, then the keyword phrase "German Shepherd Dog" would be much better than just "Dog". A few useful websites that deal with different issues regarding keywords are:

- KeyWordDiscovery.com: offers information regarding the popularity of certain keywords.

- KeywordDensity.com: check your sites keyword density.

- FreeKeywords.WordTracker.com: allows you to track what people are searching on search engines (daily info only).

- Adwords.google.com/select/keywordtoolexternal: measures keyword searches by the month

There are literally hundreds if not thousands of SEO companies out there. The differences in these services vary greatly. Many of these companies charge a recurring monthly fee to optimize your website. Many of the 'free' website building sites actually offers SEO as a premium service. A friend of mine recently used software by Intuit to build his site. It cost him absolutely nothing to build the site, however, if he wanted it optimized in any way, he had to pay a monthly fee. In his case, this monthly fee starts at $120 per month.

These are the primary issues you need to understand when dealing with your website. If you actually sell things on your site, then you should probably find a recent book on e-commerce sites. A good book I use for reference is "ClickStarts: Design and Launch an e-Commerce Business in a Week" by Jason Rich & Entrepreneur Press. This book is a little older than I would usually recommend (copyrighted back in 2008), however many of the principles remain relevant today. One thing I would like to note with this book, and even with my book, is while the content may still be relevant for years to come, the websites referenced often come and go. So while many of these sites I list are very good resources in 2014, they may not be in 2019. This is not necessarily true across the board for all sites, but it is something to keep in mind.

Justin's Two-Cents:

"**V**isit WebsiteOptimization.com to see how fast your web pages load."

TRUE STORY

One of the last SEO companies I dealt with charged between $200-300 per month. This particular company guaranteed I would pop up on the first page of Google results for certain keyword searches. I am not sure how exactly they were able to guarantee this, but they did.

These companies will quote many of the keyword metrics they obtain from the same sources and sites I quoted in this book. For example, they will tell you how many times someone has searched "Nail Salon Tulsa" or "sushi restaurant Phoenix" in a given month. Their sales pitch

Justin's Two-Cents:

"TopSEOs.com rates, reviews and ranks the different SEO companies, as well as direct-mail and email campaign services."

is that if you are not on the first page of search results, you may be missing out on hundreds or thousands of potential leads per month. If you find a reputable company, they are usually worth their fees.

HELPFUL HINTS

- Always be sure to include opt-in boxes on every page of your site. This allows you to capture the contact info of each lead that visits your site. You will have to entice people to opt-in by giving something away for free, such as more info, a free report or a newsletter of some sort. People are becoming ever more protective of their contact info, especially email addresses.

- Go to www.AnyBrowser.com to see how your website looks on all browsers.

NOTES: _____

_____

_____

_____

_____

_____

_____

_____

_____

_____

_____

_____

_____

_____

_____

_____

_____

_____

_____

_____

_____

_____

_____

_____

_____

_____

_____

_____

Advertising and Promoting Your Business on the Internet

We live in a very unique era, where many business owners have been in business since before the advent of the internet. This group is made up of mostly Baby-Boomers and Generation 'X'ers. Yet at the same time, the Generation 'Y'ers and Millennials, whom have grown up with the internet at their side, are old enough to own their own businesses as well. This section should help you understand how to embrace the internet to increase interest in your business and, hopefully, boost your sales regardless of which group you happen to be in.

The internet should not be as intimidating as we make it out to be. On the surface, you should treat the internet as just another media outlet. It has the power to reach the masses. This factor is multiplied significantly if something goes 'viral'. This can be a great thing for a business, or it can be a business' worst nightmare. I hope to help you learn how to use the internet to benefit your business. Many business owners, who are not entirely familiar with how the internet works, have taken the approach of simply ignoring it. This approach can be devastating.

Review Sites

There are several sites that publicly post reviews from consumers, which are intended to be used as a guide for other potential consumers. A few of these sites as of this writing, are GlassDoor, Yelp, and Angie's List. Google Places even has a business review and ranking system. Even if you, as a business owner, are

Justin's Two-Cents:

"**A** few of the other sites where reviews on business can be found are:

> **Google+ Local**
> **Yahoo Local**
> **Citysearch**
> **Insider Pages**
> **TripAdvisor**
> **Urbanspoon**
> **OpenTable**
> **Better Business Bureau**
> **PissedConsumer.com**
> **RipoffReport.com.**"

completely ignorant of the internet, you can be sure the internet is not ignorant of your business. Wouldn't you want the opportunity to address a disgruntled customer who has had a negative experience with your company? Many people have these negative experiences and take to the internet with their complaint. If you are not actively reviewing the feedback your company is getting from these review sites, then you have no idea what the public perception of your business is. These sites allow the customer to voice their opinion anonymously, and without confrontation, with the click of a mouse.

I have networked with several business owners who have similar stories of a customer visiting their business and the staff believing the person had a positive experience. Then, two weeks later they discover that same customer had posted a complaint on a popular review site within 48 hours of the experience! Some people do not want to cause a public scene, but still want their voice to be heard. Unfortunately, this is especially true if it involves a negative experience. Ever notice how most customers usually only voice their opinion if it is in the form of a complaint?

If you do not make a profile for your business on these sites, chances are someone else will. Your company could have a profile and multiple reviews on one of these sites right now, and you could be totally oblivious to it. It is not like the BBB, where, after you receive a complaint, they contact you for a response. These forums are open. One of the things you need to look out for is the opportunity for someone who has not even visited your business to post fraudulent complaints or negative reviews (maybe a competitor, or personal enemy, etc...). I have actually seen this happen many times. Bottom line is you always want to be in the know of what is being publicized concerning your business. With the ubiquitousness of the internet and these review sites, it is mandatory that a business owner be aware.

One last thing I would like to note here, there is a newer mobile app that was released out of beta in 2013 called OwnerListens. This app is available on smartphones utilizing iOS and Android as of this writing. The app allows customers the chance to send feedback to business owners anonymously via text message or online. I would recommend placing a sign in your business that briefly mentions the app, what it does, and actually encourages customers to engage with you in this manner. If there is a legitimate complaint and you do something to correct it, you may even turn that customer into your biggest advocate. This gives you a chance to nip the complaint in the bud before it has a chance to be broadcast to the entire world. Remember, when your entire business is based upon customer feedback, it pays to listen.

Internet Ads

I recently read a statistic from a survey performed by the Boston Consulting Group that surveyed 550 small businesses. The survey discovered that small business owners only spent 3 cents out of every marketing dollar on digital advertising. This seems opposite of the direction that society is heading, especially with the amount of online traffic higher now than it has ever been. Common sense would dictate you go where the consumers are going. Advertising online can be a very profitable avenue, but just like anything else, it has to be done right.

There are a few different ways to use internet ads. When you mention internet ads, most people automatically think of the annoying pop-up ads that are everywhere on the internet. This is one type of ad that I do not recommend using. These ads are despised by many, they are not perceived as credible by the general public. For the purposes of this chapter I will focus on two of the most popular internet advertising platforms: Facebook and Google.

Facebook Ads

Have you ever noticed when you log-in to Facebook there are ads displayed down the right side of the page or in your news feed? These ads were targeted specifically for you using your personal information saved in your profile. Facebook allows businesses to display ads to users based on a demographic profile. This is a very good advertising medium that many businesses either do not know about, or do not take seriously.

Ads on Facebook contain a graphic, a title, a message and a display URL. For the title of the ad, you are limited to a short phrase of usually up to about 30 characters, or so. For the ad's message you will also have a limited amount of characters. You need to word your ad with fewer characters than are available in a standard text message. In fact, this is how I come up with my ads. I first enter the message into a text message in my phone. You are limited to the amount of characters, but it is still plenty to say all that needs to be said. Then I try to trim it down without losing any pertinent information. I do this until I cut the amount of characters in half. This allows you to get everything down first, then condense it from there. Several internet advertising platforms limit you to 70 characters or so.

You will start by searching for and uploading a picture or graphic that will grab the attention of your target audience. Make sure the picture is appropriate. Facebook screens all ads before they go live and regularly rejects ads they do not think are tasteful. It is important that this graphic relates to your business in some sense. If the relation is not plainly evident, then you should tie it in with the title.

Also, keep in mind that you can appeal to different subsets within your demographic. For example, when I owned my teeth whitening clinic, I went through many different ads to see which themes worked and which ones did not. The graphic I had the most success with was a picture of a woman smiling, showing off her pearly whites. I would run the same ad four different times with the only difference being the model in the graphic being of different ethnic background.

Next, you need to come up with your title. It is imperative that you make this title catchy. Remember, people are on Facebook for a myriad of reasons, none of which are to be advertised to. You need to sidetrack them. You will go through many different ads to see which themes work and which ones do not. The most successful title I came up with was: "Tired of Stripping?". This was, of course, a play on words referring to the popular teeth whitening strips that I was in competition with. This title, as you can imagine, snagged people's attention because they were curious to see if I was referring to a profession as an exotic dancer.

After choosing a title, move on to the message portion of the ad otherwise known as the description. The same rules apply here as they do in other traditional advertising avenues. You need to keep it concise. Many entrepreneurs have a hard time with brevity when it comes to their business. They have so much they would like to say that it becomes hard for them to sum it all up. The problem in advertising is, since you are sidetracking your audience, you need to get to the point as quickly as possible. People do not want to, nor will they, read a narrative. If you are not a good writer then you should find someone who is. Your message needs to be condensed without removing any pertinent information.

Now you are ready to enter your display URL. This is the web address that is displayed within the ad. The link can be to any webpage of your choosing. Once a person clicks on your ad, they are delivered to whatever webpage you previously selected. For example, if your web address is www.TvFrameStore.com, you may not want to enter that as the link since that would take them to the homepage and require further work to find what the ad promised.

Instead, you may want to enter www.TvFrameStore.com/productinfo, as this may directly link to the page that has the product the ad mentioned. You can even have them directed to your company's Facebook page or even an entire different site altogether. However, as a general rule of thumb, take these people directly to the product or service mentioned in the ad. They have successfully responded to the ad, so don't make them do more work once they click on the ad.

For those who are not internet-savvy, here are step-by-step directions on how to do this:

- Keep the browser window open that you are developing the ad on (window #1)

- Open a second browser window (window #2)

- In window #2, navigate to the exact webpage you want people delivered to once they click on your ad.

- Now highlight the entire URL and copy it

- Go back to window #1 and paste the URL in the box that asks where you want to send people to once they click on your ad (this may be called the Display URL)

The next thing you need to do is select a target demographic that you would like your ad displayed to. You need to narrow the field, so to speak. Is your target customer male or female? What age range are you shooting for? If you are already in business, then you should already know this. If you are new to business, then you will quickly learn this is something you need to figure out ASAP. (see previous chapter, "Understanding Demographics")

How to Build Your Audience on Facebook

Search for people, places and things   Home   Find Friends   Justin

Advertise on Facebook

Over 1 billion people. We'll help you reach the right ones.

Create an Ad

For free first time setup service
Call 1-800-601-0077
or request a callback

Overview
How it Works
Success Stories
State Bicycle Co.
Luxury Link
Top Questions

1. Build a Facebook Page
✓ Add a unique cover photo and use your logo as a profile picture
✓ Create a post so when people visit your Page they see recent activity
✓ Make sure to like your Page and share it with your friends

Create a Page

2. Connect to your fans with ads
✓ Create multiple ads to help build an audience for your Page
✓ Use the targeting options to show your ads to only the people you want reach
✓ See which versions of your ads work best

3. Engage your fans with great content on your Page
✓ Add a new post to your Page at least once a week
✓ Pin your most important posts to the top of your Page
✓ Ask questions, share exclusive news and respond to people when they post or comment on your Page

4. Influence the friends of your fans
✓ Encourage check-ins, participation in events or create an offer to encourage more activity on your Page
✓ When people interact with the content on your Page, their friends are eligible to see the activity
✓ When people do things such as like, comment or check-in to your Page, you can promote those activities to their friends

Create an Ad   or contact our sales team

About   Create Ad   Create Page   Developers   Careers   Privacy   Cookies   Terms   Help

Facebook © 2013 · English (US)

Facebook users believe that every data point they enter into Facebook is just to post on their profile to share with their friends. In reality, these data points are merely clever tactics Facebook uses to carve out a demographic profile of each individual user. Their goal is to target these ads at their users as accurately as possible.

If the data point is something Facebook asks their users, then you can narrow down your field based on those criteria. For example, relationship status differentiates between married and single for advertising purposes. A few of the areas you can narrow down a demographic are by age, marital status, geographic location and education level.

Once you have selected your target demographic, you now get to make the financial decisions. There are two methods of paying for Facebook ads. Pay-per-click ads are self-explanatory. You pay each time someone clicks on your ad. Pay-per-impression ads, on the other hand, charge you every time your ad is displayed. Facebook will allow you the option of choosing which payment method you would like to use.

Pay-per-click ads are the better choice, especially when starting a new campaign. These ads are more expensive but allow your dollars only to be spent on someone interested in your business. The most common question I am asked is, "How much does it cost per-click?" The answer is different for every situation. This is entirely dependent upon the target audience you selected in the previous step. There is a complex, built-in algorithm that adjusts the price using simple supply and demand principles. If you have selected a highly sought after audience, then you will have to pay more per-click. A general range you can expect to pay is $.75-$1.25 per-click, as of this writing. The actual price you pay will vary. They will actually ask what your bid price is. They will make a recommendation. I would advise going with the recommended bid price.

I used Facebook ads to advertise to women in my area that were between the ages of 19-45. In some campaigns (more on campaigns in a bit) I chose only women that had a college education. In some campaigns I chose only single women. The different campaigns fluctuated between $.76-$1.07 per click.

The other payment method is pay-per-impression. This method charges you every time your ad is displayed. This is more of a shotgun approach. You show this ad to a bunch of people that fit your demographic and hope a lot of them like what they see. The only time this method is more sensible is if you have a high rate of clicks compared to the amount of impressions you have. If you choose this method of advertising, selecting an accurate target demographic becomes much more important.

The next thing you get to do is set a daily budget. In other words, you can lay out how much are you willing to spend each day. This can be as little as $10. For example, let's say you run two different ads. Your average click for each ad costs $1, and your daily budget is $10 per ad. Once you have ten clicks on one of the ads, it will stop displaying for that day (until midnight). The second ad will still run if it has not yet hit its daily max budget. This limits your downside. With a single ad with a daily budget of $10, you are guaranteed to never spend more than $310 on any given month. However, this also limits your exposure. The best thing to do is to set a budget that you can afford. No more and no less.

Now on to campaigns. When developing your ads, especially if you are new to internet advertising, you need to test different methods. Create several different ads with different titles and messages and possibly even send people to different URLs. These ads are differentiated through separate campaigns. You can try tweaking the demographic to reach different audiences. For example, you can use a specific graphic, title, and message for ads targeting an African-American base as opposed to a Hispanic base. The same principle applies for campaigns targeting men as opposed to women. By separating these into different campaigns you can track the analytics easily.

Facebooks 'Campaigns and Ads' dashboard is very organized and allows you to track your ads and campaigns performance in real time. Some of the analytics you can track are the cost-per-click (CPC), click-through-rate (CTR), number of clicks and number of impressions. This allows you to be able to test different ads and track their performance, (see example in previous chapter: 'Tracking Your Advertising Efforts').

Conversion Tracking

Search for people, places and things   Home ↑   Find Friends   Justin

| **Ads Manager** | **Conversion Tracking** | **Create Conversion Pixel** |

Account

Justin Bicket

Keep track of important actions people take on your website after they click or view on your ads. Learn more in the Help Center.

Get started by creating a conversion tracking pixel and placing it on your website. A pixel is a snippet of code that sends information back to Facebook when someone has viewed or clicked on your ad and then taken a specific action (ex: buying something) on your website.

Campaigns & Ads

Pages

Reports

Settings

Billing

1. Click the green button in the upper right corner of this page that says "Create Conversion Pixel".
2. Give your conversion pixel a name so it's easy for you to remember what you're tracking.
3. Choose a category - this is the name of the action you want to track on your website - and click "Create Pixel".
4. A box will appear with a JavaScript code that you'll need to paste into the code of your website. If you can add code to your website, you should paste it between <head> and </head> on the webpage where you want to track conversions. For example, if you want to track when people buy things, paste the code on the checkout confirmation page of your website. If you don't know how to add code to your website, you should ask a developer or technical person to help.

Conversion Tracking

Power Editor

When your code is working properly it will show as verified on this page. Then you're ready to create an ad and track conversions that happen on your website.

Learn More

Help

Help Community

Search your ads

Google AdWords

Google is by far the most powerful and popular search engine used today. Using Google AdWords means you can display your text-based ads on Google whenever someone enters a search word or phrase that matches the keywords you selected when designing your ad. This is assuming you are willing to pay the going rate for that particular ad at that time. I would like to note here that there are other search engines that offer similar programs, such as Yahoo! Small Business Search Engine Marketing and Microsoft AdCenter. The same principles will generally apply to them as well. I am using Google as an example because it is the most popular.

Not only can you choose to have your ads displayed to

Justin's Two-Cents:

"Many times only ten or so keywords are responsible for the lion's share of your online traffic. Identify and break down each of these top keywords into their own separate ad campaign, writing ads for each keyword individually. You should see an increase in traffic."

people performing Google searches, but Google AdWords also has a large content network as well. This content network is made up of other websites that receive a significant amount of traffic and agree to host Google AdWords ads. They agree to this because Google shares a portion of the ad revenue with them. There are literally thousands upon thousands of websites in Google's content network from all over the world.

Basically, if you choose to advertise on Google search network and Google content network, you can potentially reach millions of internet users.

Here are the steps for setting up a Google AdWords campaign:

1. Set up an account on Google Adwords. They will require a debit/credit card or PayPal account on file along with an opening deposit (usually $50-100 will do).

2. Create a detailed list of specific keywords that are directly related to your product, business or industry. Examples of these words are specific names of products and industry jargon. Think about what people would search for on Google when looking for products or services you offer. The search engines offer a set of online tools to help you build a comprehensive list of keywords. They can even forecast how many impressions your ad will receive based on your budget. You are usually allowed up to 50 keywords.

3. Create your ad. This is similar to the process outlined in the Facebook section. These ads are text-based and contain a title, message, and URL.

4. Set your daily budget and how much you are willing to pay per click. The more you are willing to pay per click, the better placement your ad will have. You may notice on Google searches there are two highlighted ads at the top of the search results, and then there are the ads that go down the right side in list form. Not only do you get prime placement, but a higher cost per-click will also increase the frequency in which your ad is

displayed.

5. Use Google Analytics to track your advertising efforts in real time.

These ads are usually billed on a per-click basis. The same pricing situation applies here as it does to Facebook. I knew a guy who had advertised on Google Adwords using pay-per-click ads. His target demographic was very limited and not highly sought after. He paid about $.30 per click. However, my dad owned an online business that sold model ships, and he paid between $.90-1.00 per-click on average.

The bottom line is: using internet ads allows you the freedom of trying a hundred different ads if you want. You can change these ads in less than five minutes, and you can experiment with different headlines, keywords and messages. These ads can all lead to the same webpage or you can try sending them to different landing pages on your site. Internet ads allow for a lot of flexibility. Try them out. Put a lot of thought into selecting your keywords and target audience. Check your analytics tools at least once per day. Constantly test, track and tweak your ads.

TRUE STORY

When I first ran ads for my teeth whitening clinic on Facebook, I tested a couple different ads. The first ad was up and running while the others were still awaiting approval from Facebook. Like a kid on Christmas, I kept checking Facebooks analytics tool that allowed me to track the number of impressions and clicks in real time. I checked this dozens of times throughout the day. I received two phone calls from women who had seen our ad on Facebook and wanted to set up an appointment. After getting off the phone with the second woman, I refreshed our analytics page. I forget how many impressions we had, but we had only three clicks on the ad. I couldn't believe it, out of the first three clicks on our ad, we netted two sales. Those three clicks only cost me about $2.70 but brought in over $250 in revenue!

Now I am not saying that everyone will experience these type of immediate results, and we certainly did not keep this ratio up in the long run. But these ads did prove to be an extremely effective advertising medium.

HELPFUL HINTS

- After you run some Facebook ads for a while, check the analytics of your more successful ads and compare the number of impressions to the number of clicks. For example, let's say you would have to pay $.01 per-impression or $1 per-click for the same ad. Find out what the ratio is of impressions compared to clicks. If you're getting more than one click for every 100 impressions, it may be worthwhile to try the same ad on a pay-per-impression basis. When you do the math, you would be getting more bang for your buck since you have a high click-through-rate. This is the only circumstance under which I would recommend running pay-per-impression ads. If you try this, you should keep up with the daily analytics to monitor these ads.

- Treat any unsuccessful ads as learning experiences and try to figure out why certain ads work and others fail. This will help you create winning ads you can then use in all of your other advertising efforts as well. If an ad copy has success under one medium, chances are you have a winner that it will succeed in other mediums as well.

- Experiment with different ad variations, using a modest budget, until you create an ad with a low cost-per-click and a high click-through rate. Once you have isolated this ad, invest the vast majority of your budget in this ad. However, keep some money aside to test new ads in search of another winner.

NOTES: _____

_____

Promoting Your Business with Social Media

Social media allows for an awesome opportunity for small businesses to connect with their prospective customers on a personal and social level. Unfortunately, most small businesses misuse, and even abuse, this powerful medium. This effectively turns those prospects off. Once this happens, it is extremely difficult to recover from.

Fortunately, it is surprisingly simple to correct mistakes made while promoting your business on social media. It simply takes a change of perspective. I will touch on the most popular social media platforms. Some of my examples and hypothetical scenarios use Facebook. However, the underlying principles are applicable across the board to other social media site as well.

The number of one mistake businesses make is marketing too aggressively. My friend and mentor, Kevin Simmonds, said it best, "People are on Facebook to be social, not to be sold to." Facebook is a site where people are there to connect, build relationships, and interact with friends. Be casual and informational. Take the soft sell approach when dealing with people on social media. You must be subtle to successfully promote your business on Facebook. As soon as your business connects with a new person on Facebook, you should send them a message thanking them, BRIEFLY describe what your business does, and inform them of any specials you may have. Leave it up to them to ask for more information if they would like it. You should regularly post pictures of your products, satisfied customers and any articles related to your business or industry

that your followers may find interesting. This is not to say you can never promote a special via social sites, but 80% of your efforts should be informational.

I have networked with mechanics that tweet daily tips regarding preventative maintenance and automotive tips. I know photographers that post their work on Facebook and Pinterest.

I also know tattoo artists that post pictures of their latest masterpieces on Instagram. Remember, Instagram is primarily for raw, unedited images. In fact, most pictures on Instagram are quick snapshots taken by smartphones. If photos help promote your offerings, then social media sites can be a great place to showcase.

I would also recommend encouraging your customers to use social media to openly, and honestly communicate about their experiences with your

Justin's Two-Cents:

On Twitter:

- **Use hashtags that are currently trending to encourage engagement from those who are not your followers.**
- **Tweet a question. It invokes people to think, and then respond.**
- **Use line breaks. They allow your tweet to take up a larger portion of the phone screen and attract more attention.**

On Pinterest:

- **Place your most important pins as close to the middle of the page on the first or second row. Research shows that pins placed front and center receive more attention.**
- **According to Pinerly, pins that contain a call to action experience an 80% increase in engagement.**
- **In the Pinterest settings page, verify your website to gain access to the Web Analytics feature. This way you can track which pins are paying off.**

Justin's Two-Cents:

- **On Facebook's top brand pages, videos are shared 12 times more often than text and links?**
- **Instagram is growing faster than Facebook**
- **45 million photos are uploaded to Instagram each day**
- **Pinterest refers more traffic to outside websites than Twitter**
- **When you share a comment on LinkedIn, you are sharing it with everyone in their network, which is great for marketing**
- **Almost 50% of online shoppers worldwide rely on social media sites to assist them in making purchasing decisions (according to Nielsen.com)**
- **The four largest social media sites, in order, are: Facebook, Twitter, LinkedIn & Pinterest**
- **Its best to connect with people on social media within 24 hours of meeting them in real life.**

company. This transparency gives you an air of credibility. If someone posts something negative about your business on their profile, be diplomatic and attempt to fix the problem and make the customer happy. Others will see this extraordinary customer service effort, and likely view your company in a positive light.

One of the best things you can do is post daily tips or helpful hints. Anything that your followers would find interesting or important would make for a good post. Then encourage any kind of feedback. I like the idea of posting an open-ended question. It's a way to be interactive without sounding to pushy or pitchy.

LinkedIn is different from Facebook. LinkedIn is a social site strictly for businessmen and women who want to connect with other business professionals. Many members even post their resumes, which can be viewed by others. You can also tap into the business contacts of other business professionals, and build a mighty Rolodex in the process. LinkedIn is great for networking, as well as B2B sales. It's very useful for those in professional services, such as CPAs, business attorneys, and insurance agents.

There is a unique feature on LinkedIn called 'Answers'. Members can log into the forum and answer questions others have posted. Answering these questions is a good way to gain recognition as an expert in your field. I would like to note here that they do assign scores based upon the quality of your answers, so make sure you know what you're talking about before posting any answers.

TRUE STORY

I was once one of those business owners that sent out tons of messages to our followers on Facebook. Always mentioning our services, special offers and promotions. I suffered from the same ignorance that plagues many other business owners. I was on Facebook to sell, sell, sell. Then a mentor of mine helped me step back and think like a consumer.

On my personal Facebook page, I was friends with a local pub. They sent me special event notifications, happy hour and drink specials, and many other advertisements on a regular basis. I soon became numb to them. Whenever I would receive a notification from them, I would just ignore it. This is what we, as consumers, do: we train our brains to ignore advertisements.

Justin's Two-Cents:

Some Useful Social Media Tools.

- **IFTTT (If this then that) automates tasks such as creating Facebook updates when someone checks in via Foursquare, or auto-saving photos to DropBox.**
- **SocialOomph can schedule tweets, or auto-follow those who follow you on Twitter.**
- **dlvr.it can schedule and autopost to several platforms at once.**
- **Sprout Social & Kapow software incorporate all social media platforms into one easy-to-use dashboard.**
- **BlkDot allows you to embed a subtle black 'Buy' button on Tumblr photos. It also allows you to cross post the link to other social media platforms. They charge you 3% of each transaction and works in conjunction with Stripe's merchant-processing service.**
- **Stipple allows photos to be tagged with your company info, no matter where the picture is shared on the web.**

Long story short, instead I started posting daily informational bits related to our industry. This was the first time I had any positive customer engagement using social media. Eventually, people were looking forward to our daily tips post. This is how you embrace the power of social media. Social media is a share-of-mind medium, but too many business use it as if it were a share-of-market medium. Do not go into social media with the idea of converting prospects into customer right away. This may happen, but it should not be your goal.

HELPFUL HINTS

Ever wonder if anyone is talking about your business online? Whether it is positive or negative banter, I do not know any business owner who would not like to know what is being said about their company. It just so happens that there are sites you can go to in order to check this.

- For Twitter: Monitter.com allows you to enter your company's name, or Twitter username, and it will show you anything and everything that has been posted mentioning your company on Twitter.

- For blogs: Google.com/alerts allows you to enter the keywords you would like to be alerted to, and they will email you a daily list of blog sites that are discussing those keywords.

Bonus Pinterest Section

"**P**interest is all about creating and 'pinning' graphics or pictures that are useful, educational and inspiring. Once again, the same concept applies to Pinterest as with all other social media platforms: be informational.

You are there to educate. Try to abide by the 80/20 rule: 80% of your pins should be educational an inspiring, 20% should be promotive. You can effectively incorporate more text in a pin than you can in a tweet or Facebook post. Especially if your infographic is designed right. Infographics are simply graphics or pictures with supporting text in the same frame.

Many people are shopping while on Pinterest. They will spend more time reading your content here than they would with any other advertisement, or even on Facebook for that matter. You should also incorporate Pinterest with your other social media efforts. Create a Pinterest tab on Facebook. Tweet your pins. You can even embed your pins in your blog posts.

You need to plan out what your goal is for each pin. Nothing too in-depth, but a general idea. Are you trying to boost sales, drive traffic to your website, encourage customer engagement, or just simply let people know you exist in the marketplace? Naturally, you want to match your pins with their intended purpose, just as you would with any other advertisement.

Pinterest has a 'Pin it' button you can install on your website. This is highly recommended. You can also designate a feature image for each webpage and blog post. This image can be immediately pinned with no further work. You should also install a 'Follow me on Pinterest' button on the homepage of your website. You want to create a pin-friendly experience to anyone visiting your site.

Just as with other social media platforms, you can 're-pin', 'comment' or 'like' other pins. This is great for exposure. You can interact with others without trying to sell to them. This is all about establishing yourself as an industry expert. You should also incorporate appropriate keywords in your pins and descriptions. This will help boost your search engine ranking. A good trick is to use hashtags to highlight keywords and phrases that your prospects commonly search for."

Daily Deal Sites

The recession of 2008 helped bring about this entirely new and innovative marketing medium. Daily deal sites, such as Groupon and Living Social, have become household names in a relatively short period of time. These sites became popular by their dual-headed approach. First, they offered consumers great bargains at local businesses. Secondly, they boosted (discounted) sales for these local businesses in an economically tough time.

For those who are unfamiliar with how these sites work, allow me to break it down for you. These sites have a large email database of dedicated users. They send out a daily promotional email once per day to the members in that database. This promotion usually features a local business, and offers a wildly large discount on a product or service. The deals can be purchased during that day only, as they usually expire at midnight and a new business is featured the next day. (Note: recently, they have moved away from this by making the deals available for several

 **Justin's Two-Cents:**

Daily Deal Sites:

Groupon.com

LivingSocial.com

OfficeArrow.com

GroupPrice.com

MarketSharing.com

BizyDeal.com

MarketBlitzDeals.com

days).

These sites are known for selling a large volume of these deals. There is no up-front fee for featuring your businesses promotion on these sites. The deals are sold through the daily deal website and the customer prints out a voucher to bring into your business. The vouchers have bar codes and

Justin's Two-Cents:

"**W**hen people call or stop by your store on the day of the promotion, encourage them to purchase the deal there on the spot, in person or over the phone. This way you can keep 100% of the purchase price. This can help increase your profit margins."

unique serial numbers on them so they can't be duplicated. At the end of the promotion, the site will email you a customer list.

Sounds fantastic on the surface, doesn't it? Well there is a bit of a catch. First, to qualify to be a featured business, you must offer at least 50% off of a product, service or gift card. If you offer a specific product or service, they prefer that you offer your best-selling product or service. If the products retail price is $100, you have to give at least a $50 discount. After the discount, this leaves a $50 purchase price. Then the daily deal site wants half of the purchase price. This would leave you with $25 in revenue for a $100 product. It is important to note here that the percentage the daily deal site takes is negotiable. You should be able to negotiate a deal where they only take 30-40% of the purchase price. I recently read an article in a business magazine that said the average cut these daily deal sites take is around 35-37%.

These promotions tend to be fairly successful. Most of these sites allow you to set a minimum amount of deals that have to be sold in order for the promotion to take effect. The rep informed me that this is basically a gimmick intended to get people to purchase these deals and encourage others to purchase them. They set a quota at an easily attainable number. They also allow you to set a maximum amount of deals you would like sold. This may be important if you operate a

Justin's Two-Cents:

"**A**pproximately 30-40% of the people who purchase your deal will redeem the voucher within 30 days of the sale. So plan accordingly. Expect an influx of new customers with lots of questions. It pays to have an extra person or two around, especially on the first day of your promotion."

business that does not have high profit margins and would like to put a cap on the amount of these deals that are available.

I know of several restaurants that use these sites to drum up business during slow times. Restaurant profit margins tend to be lower than a lot of other businesses, which is why you will usually see a restaurant sell a $20 gift card for $10. This minimizes their downside. This is a very popular deal for a restaurant. They will end up losing money if every customer that comes in to redeem the deal doesn't spend any additional money. Usually these businesses try to upsell customers when they visit the business.

The sales pitch these daily deal sites use to get businesses to sign up is very boilerplate. Suppose they have a current subscriber base, in your area, of 140,000 users. Obviously you won't sell nearly that many deals. However, after running a promotion, all 140,000 of those people will now know your business exists. When you mention that your business can't survive off of 25-35% of your normal retail prices, they have a counter for that. They will tell you that you are giving people a tremendous value to visit your business. Many of these people will be first time customers and would not have normally visited your business, but for this promotion. They are helping get new customers in your door, and now the onus is on you to give those people a great experience and turn them into repeat customers.

These promotions can be very enticing since there is no up-front capital investment on your part. They can even have the appearance of being very profitable. For most businesses, though, this is not a feasible marketing medium to be used regularly.

The daily deal site will have a payment schedule worked out in a contract before your deal is featured. They usually divide your cut into thirds. You receive a check for the first third within a week of your promotions feature. The second third comes after thirty days. The final installment being after sixty days.

Justin's Two-Cents:

"These sites are not an all-in-one marketing approach. Do not become dependent on these deals. By constantly discounting your products, you devalue your products in the eye of your customers and prospective customers."

There are exceptions to this, though. For example, after a couple successful features with Groupon, I signed an exclusive agreement with them. The terms of this agreement were that they would allow us to run a promotion once per quarter, if we wanted. They also would send us a check for 90% of our cut within one week of the promotion being featured, with the remaining 10% being sent after thirty days. On my end, I had to agree to be exclusive with Groupon and not use any of their direct competitors.

These promotions can be a very good tool that can generate a lot of revenue in a short period of time. However, this is not for every business, as these deals eat away at your margins. Lately I have read many articles discussing the problems many businesses are experiencing by relying solely on daily deal sites as their only advertising efforts. This is clearly not sustainable. For a new business owner, or one that is not accounting-savvy, running these deals regularly may give the illusion of profitability. However, it is hard to be profitable without profit margins.

TRUE STORY

I tried out three different daily deal sites to feature my teeth whitening clinic.

As it turns out, teeth whitening services do rather well on these sites. The first site we were featured on resulted in a dismal response. We sold 16 deals on this site. This site was new at the time and ran by the city newspaper.

The second site was Living Social, and was the second most popular site (in terms of users) in our area at the time. We sold 46 deals with them. This was a decent return, since our price point was $99. However, it was not as good as we had hoped for, or were told to expect.

The last site we tried was Groupon. The first time we were featured on Groupon, we sold 168 deals at $149 each. I had negotiated a 60/40 split with them, where I kept $90 out of each deal, minus a 1.25% credit card processing fee. We ran this deal at the end of October in our first year of business. We hoped to get some holiday gift purchasers. We brought in a little under $15,000 from this deal.

We ran the same deal after the holidays during a generally slow time for retail in late January. We sold 227 deals that go-around. While it was great for exposure, it killed our margins. I should note here, the margins in teeth whitening are rather high. Our packages sold for $99-299. Our product cost was between $10-19 for any of these packages. However, after running some numbers, I realized that the package we sold for $149 on the site, took three hours of our time, leaving us with about $25 per hour after figuring in product cost. Now you can see why this was not sustainable in the long run.

HELPFUL HINTS

- When you run these promotions, the rep from the daily deal site will likely tell you to have extra staff on hand to answer phone calls, emails, and questions posted on the sites forum. I thought they were exaggerating when they told me this. They were not. I was flooded with calls, emails and questions. It pays to have an extra person or two around, especially on the first day of your promotion.

- Ask about running your deal on a Friday. Oftentimes, your deal will be featured throughout the entire weekend if it is featured on a Friday. Whereas deals on a weekday usually expire at midnight. Some sites have shied away from ending these deals at midnight, offering the deals for several days at a time. However, the original model called for the deals to expire at midnight, therefore creating a sense of urgency for people to buy these deals. They are really targeted at consumers making impulse buys.

- These sites will usually try to get you to agree to deducting about 2-3% out of your cut for credit card processing fees. This is also negotiable. For example, Groupon wanted me to deduct 2.5% of the total sale, out of my end. I argued they should be responsible for paying this. We ended up splitting the difference, with me paying 1.25%

- 10-20% of the deals sold never get redeemed. When the Groupon rep told me this, I thought this an exaggerated sales tactic. Even if it were true on the average deal, since our price point was so high ($149), I thought

Justin's Two-Cents:

These sites can be used to drum up business during a slow season or for a grand opening. However, you must be careful when you structure these deals. I will use the restaurant example mentioned earlier, since their margins are notoriously low. Let's say you own a restaurant and your average ticket is around $40. Do not give a $40 gift card for $20. If you did this, under the best case scenario, you will collect 30% of your normal retail price ($12 out of $40).

Instead, offer a $20 gift card for $10. This way, on average, you will only lose 60-70% on HALF of the average bill. You will receive 100% payment for the other half of the bill not covered by the promotion. This way you end up with 65% of that average ticket ($26 out of $40).

we would have a much higher rate of redemption. After all, not too many people will throw away $149, right? Turns out about 10-20% of our deals were never redeemed. I couldn't believe it. You track this by entering the customers voucher number into Groupons analytics database.

NOTES: _____

_____

_____

_____

_____

_____

_____

_____

_____

_____

_____

_____

_____

_____

_____

_____

_____

_____

_____

Networking

Throughout this book, you will see many examples used that mention networking with other business owners. This is a great idea particularly if you network with other business owners who have the same demographic customer base as you. Learning what has and has not worked for businesses similar to yours can be invaluable knowledge. This allows you the opportunity to learn lessons that would otherwise cost you thousands of dollars to learn.

I once discussed the idea of advertising in a local women's magazine, with the owner of a medspa that was next-door to my store. She explained to me that a little over a year prior, she thought it would be a great idea to advertise in this same magazine. She signed a one-year contract with them and was disappointed with the results. She said they tracked their advertising, and had received 2-3 leads that mentioned seeing their ad in that magazine during the entire year.

After checking with several other business owners who were also in the

> ## Justin's Two-Cents:
>
> "**W**hen attending networking meetings, it is important to bring a stack of business cards. The members usually keep a small stack of each other's business cards to pass on to people they may refer to you. "

elective cosmetic services business, I found that everyone who had advertised with this magazine felt the same way. I never did find a business owner who was satisfied with the results from advertising in this magazine, but I never surveyed all their current advertisers either.

There are networking groups established in nearly every metropolitan area. All it takes is for you to Google: "[your city] small business networking groups", to find local listings. This is also a major function of the Chamber of Commerce. There are other groups, such as B.N.I., that are dedicated small business networking groups with several chapters in each city. These groups usually require you to become a member by paying an annual fee and attending weekly meetings. They are only as valuable as you make them. The members at these meetings commonly pass referrals and leads on to each other.

Some of these groups only want one member from each field. For example, they will have one insurance agent, one photographer, one eye doctor, etc... per chapter. This becomes very important when it comes to passing leads. Let's say an accountant has a sister that is getting married soon. The accountant would most likely refer the sister to the photographer in her networking group for the wedding photos.

In return if the photographer ever needs an accountant or knows anyone who many need one, they would most likely pass the lead back to the accountant. You can quickly see how effective these groups can be at promoting each other's businesses.

Not all business owners are the outgoing, sociable type or may be too busy to attend these meetings. In these cases it is best to send a company representative that represents your company at these meetings. Sort of like a brand ambassador. This person has to be a go-getter. This person

Justin's Two-Cents:

"**B**e on the lookout for fusion-marketing partners you could possibly partner with in the future. These are other businesses with similar prospects and customer bases."

would preferably be good at sales as well as be very personable.

There is also a website called Meetup.com that is a social networking site with a bit of a quirk to it. It is designed to assist people in organizing special interest groups in their area. These groups meet in person. There is currently an example of one at www.meetup.com/smallbiz-997/. This is a small business networking group for Knoxville, TN. The organizer of this group is Jonathan Taylor, author of "The Official Small Business Guide to Marketing 2.0". He discusses in his book how the members, who are all entrepreneurs, share strategies that work in their respective industries. This can be a very valuable tool if used correctly.

You should check Meetup's site to see if they have any groups like this in your area. You should also check with your local Chamber of Commerce as well as performing Google searches to find groups in your area. If, after all of this, you still can't find one: start one yourself and set up a profile for the group on Meetup.com.

> ## Justin's Two-Cents:
>
> "Two good sites to write down are:
>
> Icewbo.org: International Chambers of Commerce
>
> Uschamber.co: United States Chambers of Commerce"

TRUE STORY

I attended two different meetings for two different networking groups to try them out. Before leaving the first meeting, I had two leads that both turned into paying customers. I also witnessed at least 20-30 leads being exchanged. I have to admit, I was a little skeptical of these meetings before I showed up. After one hour, I learned so much from these other business owners that had been in business for many years. They had made it where many others had failed. This is not something to be taken lightly. I learned much of what I know about small business marketing by absorbing info from the multitude of business owners and entrepreneurs I have networked with since then.

HELPFUL HINTS

- When you're new to these groups, try to be proactive in giving referrals. The members of these networking groups have such a great kinship. They will go out of their way to send you some business in return. Everyone is trying scratch each other's back, in a sense. Each of the members understands and appreciates how valuable a new customer is to their business and reciprocates this very well. If, by chance, you attend one of these meetings and do not get that vibe, search out another group.

- When attending networking events, go with the intention of being social and having a good time meeting new people, not with the intention of making money. Trying to advertise to everyone and constantly talking about your business will turn people off. Instead listen to others and try to help them solve any problems they may have. Also, collect as many business cards as you can.

- Make sure you follow up with everyone you meet at a networking event.

NOTES: _____

_____

_____

_____

_____

_____

_____

_____

_____

_____

_____

_____

_____

_____

_____

_____

Television Advertising

Technology has affected TV advertising for the better, and for the worse. It has adversely affected advertising in the form of the DVR. For those who do not know, a DVR allows you to record TV programming for later viewing. This allows the viewers an opportunity to fast-forward through commercials. Since TV advertising is what provides the revenue for the programs and shows to air, some argue that DVR is counterproductive technology.

On a positive note, TV advertising has come a long way in terms of affordability and accessibility for small businesses. This is due to the proliferation and constant expansion of cable and satellite TV. The production costs have gone down considerably, as well as the price of the TV spots themselves. As a side note, whenever I refer to cable TV, the same principles apply to satellite as well. The cable networks have hundreds of channels, each targeting different niches. Since the entire viewing audience is spread out over such a wide range of specialty stations, it gives small business owners two distinct advantages.

First, it allows you to be very specific as to the types of audiences you want to reach. For example, Lifetime, TLC, Oxygen and OWN may be networks to look into if you are targeting women. If you are targeting male sports fans, you have SPEED, G4, SPIKE and ESPN, to name a few. It seems as if cable and satellite TV constantly come up with new, niche stations. Furthermore, specialty reality TV shows have become more popular. As of this writing, there are shows based solely on real estate investing (Flipping Vegas; Flip or Flop), comic book collecting (Comic Book Men), pawn broking (Pawn Stars) and even shows dedicated to failing businesses (Bar Rescue; The Profit). And these are just a few examples off the top of my head. This allows you to target your demographic with much more precision.

Secondly, it reduces the cost of running each commercial. You pay by how many households your ad is shown to. Since people have many more options for channels, naturally, you will have fewer viewers on each station. This, in turn, makes the cost of running your commercial cheaper, while narrowing your viewership to a more specific demographic than was ever previously imagined with TV. Oftentimes, you can also select which cities, suburbs and even neighborhoods in which your ad is displayed to.

> ## Justin's Two-Cents:
>
> "**A**ccording to Nielsen Media Research, each year, from 2010 – 2013, the average American watched more than five hours of TV every day. (154-158 hours per month.)"

For example, if you owned a comic book store, you would most likely benefit by running commercial spots during episodes of Comic Book Men. This is such a highly specific niche that would have been hard to hit with such precision even five years ago. This is just one example. The underlying principle is applicable across the board. If you run a home inspection service, you have house-flipping shows. If you own a thrift store, you have Storage Wars and American Pickers. You get the point.

Just how much have these rates dropped? Well, in Omaha, Nebraska, between 2011-2014, you could purchase thirty-second spots on the Oxygen network for $2 each. These rates were obviously higher for more popular stations and programming. For example, running a thirty-second commercial during a new episode of the Tyra Banks Show, was around $30. I know this sounds extremely affordable, but this can be deceiving. When you pay a small amount for your ad to run, expect it to be shown to a small audience. How much you pay is relative to the size of the viewing audience.

If you have a very specific target audience, chances are you can really benefit from advertising on cable networks. The ideal scenario for any marketing medium is to advertise to as much of your target audience as possible, while not wasting a dime advertising to people outside of your demographic. This is, of course, virtually impossible. However, sometimes you can get as close to this ideal as possible using cable advertising. If done correctly, you can avoid paying for a lot of wasted coverage.

Justin's Two-Cents:

"If you are interested in running a direct-response ad campaign on cable TV, ask the network rep if you can run your ad on a per-inquiry or per-sale basis. This way, you have no up-front fees. You only pay whatever you receive an inquiry or a sale resulting from that TV spot."

Many advertising reps will try to run the same spiel on you in an attempt to get you to sign an advertising contract with them. They will tell you their advertising medium is the best, but it's only successful if you run it over and over again. How convenient for them! For many advertising avenues this is simply not true. Remember, share-of-market advertising shoots for instant sales. However, this is true of share-of-mind advertising mediums, and TV falls under this category. TV ads are only effective if viewed several times. You need to run several spots on a regular basis to see results. This can become expensive, but if used correctly, it can be very effective. But I stress: IF USED CORRECTLY.

As a rule of thumb, television advertising is only effective if used frequently. The only exception to this rule is if you are advertising a limited-time sale, or if you are using TV as a direct-response medium. Using TV as a direct-response medium involves purchasing a time slot long enough to educate the audience of your product (usually 1-2 minutes), informing them of the special offer, and then provide the audience with the contact information they can use to make the purchase. The key is connecting these steps smoothly, and giving the audience enough information to make the decision to buy from you.

If you are not running a direct-response campaign, then you need to be patient when it comes to TV advertising. Do not expect to see instant results. Usually, you will not start seeing results before 60-90 days into your campaign. It takes a certain amount of repetition for someone to see an ad and subconsciously decide the company is credible. It is an uphill battle to gain credibility from people who are hearing about you for the first time. About one-third of the general public believes TV commercials are misleading. This is an obstacle you must overcome.

To accurately be able to determine how much TV advertising is enough to be effective, you must understand ratings. Many of you may understand what these are, but for those who do not, I will explain it for you. A gross rating point (GRP) is the equivalent of 1% of the TV households in a particular TV marketing area. The TV advertising prices are calculated based on the size of the GRPs in that marketing area. As a general rule of thumb, the minimum amount of advertising time you should consider purchasing to run an effective campaign is 140-160 GRPs per month.

For example, let's say you own a restaurant in an area that has one million TV households. One GRP would be equal to 10,000 TV households. To mount an effective campaign, you need to have your ad hit 15 million TVs in a given month. Obviously this does not mean 15 million unique TVs. You are going to have many of the same people view your ad several times throughout the month.

Let's say you are going to teach a free cooking class at your restaurant during one of its slow days. You decide to run an ad promoting this class during a show on the Food Network. Suppose the show is aired five days a week and averages 20,000 viewers in your area, per episode. Each time your commercial airs during this show, you are using 2 GRPs.

If you ran this commercial twice per episode, each of the five days, you would be running ten commercials per week, which translates to 20 GRPs. If you did this four weeks per month, then you would be airing forty commercials per month, equal to 80 GRPs. If you ran this same campaign during another show with similar ratings, you would be using 160 GRPs in a month, which falls into the higher end of the minimum target range.

As you can see, this is not a lot of advertising. Keep in mind you do not need to run these commercials everyday or even every week. Many businesses run them four days per week or 2-3 weeks out of the month. You can be as creative as you would like in coming up with the total GRPs per month.

The price of each rating point is entirely dependent on the size of your viewing area, the season, and the competitive environment you are in. Also, many entrepreneurs do not know that the rate cards these advertising sales reps use are 100% negotiable. They are merely starting points for negotiations.

Oftentimes, you can get better deals purchasing your airtime through a media-buying service. Since they buy so many blocks of airtime, they receive bulk discounts that you could not get on your own. They usually charge less than 10% of the total advertising cost. Be wary of any trying to charge more than 10%. Make sure you compare the prices for your desired campaign through both the network sales rep and the media-buying service. The media-buying service should be cheaper even after figuring in their fee.

The single most expensive part of a TV advertising campaign is the production cost. The sales rep can usually work out a decent discount for production costs if you buy a lot of advertising up-front, or make a large contractual commitment to them. I would recommend making a commitment to them for up to ninety days. You need to run your campaign this long to test its effectiveness, anyway.

Another option is to test the waters with TV advertising by running a limited-time offer. To do this effectively, you need to make a special limited-time offer available to those who mention the commercial when buying your product. Keep in mind you will be paying for production costs for a regular ad later on if you decide to run a regular ad down the road. Try to produce a regular ad with a special snippet inserted in the ad that advertises your special. You may want to look into trying to knock out producing both ads at the same time, you should be able to produce two ads in one day. To determine whether this will save you money, you need to discuss production costs with the sales rep, these vary greatly. I have seen some companies charge by the hour and other charge by the day. I have even seen some offer an affordable package for small businesses that allows them a certain amount of hours or takes for a set price.

The TV station is going to be able to provide you with all the necessary production assistance. They will do everything from write the ad, supply the camera crew, edit the ad and everything in between. However, before making the decision to allow the TV station to write your ad, make sure you view several commercials they have previously written and aired. Many times these spots all tend to look the same and can be dull. If this is true, you need to either write the spot yourself, or hire someone qualified to write it for you.

Justin's Two-Cents:

"**R**ecord a thirty-second spot with an open end, so you can always add different special offer snippets on the end of your ad, down the road. This prevents you from creating an entirely new ad just to have a special offer. This is a great tip for those wishing to test the waters with your first ad."

Obviously writing this spot yourself would be the most cost-effective route, but you need to seriously evaluate your capabilities. Be objective and honest with yourself. Entrepreneurs often let their

egos get ahead of them and think they can do this when they should really outsource it. I would not recommend this for your first ad campaign.

What you should do is create a storyboard for your commercial. A storyboard is a panel, often made of cardboard, that graphics are attached to, creating a scene sequence for the commercial. Each graphic is called a frame. These frames should represent a chronological story line of your ideal ad. A storyboard for a thirty-second commercial usually contains less than a dozen frames. This, along with a written outline, should allow the script writer to see the idea and message you wish to convey with your ad.

You can find someone qualified to write your script using guru.com, elance.com or scriptlance.com. These sites allow you to post a description of your project and then several writers will submit bids for your project. This tends to be cheaper and less time consuming than finding and cold-calling several writers for estimates.

You may even be able to trade your businesses services for these services. Remember, try to swap business services in exchange for ANY professional services your business may need ANY time you can. This beats paying their fee, plus you get full retail credit for this exchange.

Justin's Two-Cents:

"**S**uperimpose your logo in the bottom corner of the screen for the duration of the ad. This can also increase exposure to someone fast-forwarding or muting your ad."

This same principle applies to hiring acting talent for your commercial. Many business owners may be good at running their business, but they are not actors. You need to understand your limitations. Do not make the decision to cut a corner and be the actor in your commercial unless you honestly, objectively think this would be best. It would be best to run rehearsals and get objective opinions from trusted individuals watching your

rehearsal.

These rehearsals are also important for getting all the mistakes out of the way before production starts. Mistakes cost you money during production. You need to be as efficient with the production time as possible. If you are being charged by the hour, it should take less hours if you have rehearsed your commercial several times before going into production. If you are charged by the day, you should be able to get 2-3 spots produced in a single day if you are efficient with your time.

One last option that is commonly overlooked by most businesses is sponsoring a PBS program. Contact your local PBS affiliate station and inquire about sponsoring a program. They have a variety of ways you can get your name out to their audience. You can give free on-air advice related to your industry during a break. You can also provide your businesses products, services, or gift cards to be awarded to those making significant donations to the station or to be auctioned off during a fundraiser.

> **Justin's Two-Cents:**
>
> "**C**heck the Broadcasting and cable yearbook at
>
> www.bowker.com
>
> to find a directory of media outlets and contacts."

Talk with the affiliate PBS stations in your target area about creative ideas for promoting your business on their station. One of the benefits of working with a PBS station is there is not as much competition. Your business message doesn't get drowned out by twenty other businesses as it often does with running mainstream TV commercials.

TRUE STORY

Shortly after opening my first retail store, I was bombarded by over forty different advertising reps, who were all trying to talk me into signing advertising contracts with them. I was still a little green, so I told my girlfriend, who was my receptionist at the time, to schedule appointments with the reps whenever they would call and ask for me. I was exhausted from having these people try and sell to me all day long over the phone.

In our online calendar system, we had different color codes for different types of appointments. Red time blocks were for personal appointments away from the office, various shades of blue were for customer appointments and yellow was for meetings with advertisers. Ironically, the same color as caution signs.

One day, about two weeks after our grand opening, I logged into the calendar and the computer screen lit up like a yellow traffic light! Out of a 50 hour work week, I had nearly 20 hours worth of appointments with various advertising reps. Needless to say, my girlfriend started screening the calls a little more closely after that. She eventually started telling the reps I would not talk to them unless they were a paying customer. (She was great!)

Several of these reps were from the different TV stations. By the time I had met with them, I was so numb from hearing the same sales pitch from all of these reps. This experience also allowed me to see just how cutthroat these reps would be against each other. Long story short, I never ended up advertising with any of these reps, at that time. However, through the power of negotiation, I was able to talk them into producing my entire thirty-second ad for around $300 as long as I signed at least a ninety day contract. Furthermore, I was able to talk them into a significant discount for each ad spot so long as I signed that contract. This was going to give us an entire three month ad campaign for around $900 per month plus the $300 production fee.

HELPFUL HINTS

- When brainstorming ideas for a commercial, make sure your ad is visual. Meaning if someone watched your ad without sound, your story would still be clearly understood. Display your logo and business name several times throughout the ad. This can increase your chances of your message getting across to someone who is fast-forwarding or muting your ad on a DVR.

- Insist that you be present and active during the editing process of your ad. Oftentimes the editing can make or break an ad.

- Before you produce your ad, try and plan all of these special-offer snippets you would possibly use throughout the year. For example, if you are recording in April, think about what specials you may run during the Christmas season. This way you will have them ready. This kind of planning can save you a lot of production dollars down the road. You simply add these snippets to the end of your existing ad whenever you want. If you pay for production by the day this allows you to be very efficient with the time.

- Remember, effective TV marketing is simply learning which programs your target audience watches, then advertising during those shows.

- If you have a nice, professional-looking website, consider uploading actual images of web pages from your site. Maybe showing someone how to navigate from your website homepage to learn more. It's all about engagement. You want to prompt the customer to visit your website rather than trying to push them to make a hard decision to either buy your product or not. This allows them a third, softer option: to learn more about you. It's all about baby steps.

- In the beginning, treat TV advertising money as discretionary money. If you can't afford to lose it, don't do it. There are other ways to spend this money to get a faster return on your investment.

- Check out www.MySuddenLinkMedia.com for cable TV advertising on any budget.

NOTES: _____

_____

_____

_____

_____

_____

_____

_____

_____

_____

_____

_____

_____

_____

_____

_____

_____

_____

_____

_____

_____

_____

_____

_____

_____

_____

Donating Business Services to Charities and Fundraisers

One way to build a good reputation for your business and promote your business at the same time is to donate to charities and fundraisers. Many charitable organizations have very large, dedicated and loyal followings. Some of these organizations include Susan G. Komen for the Cure, Make-a-Wish Foundation, and the American Red Cross. Many of these organizations hold annual events that receive tons of publicity for the event itself as well as their sponsors. For example, Susan G. Komen is very active during the month of October because of Breast Cancer Awareness Month. One of the best ways to get your name out there is to attach it to a good cause.

Sponsoring these events can be structured in many different ways. I sponsored a banquet once that was put on by a local charity at a church. After the dinner they had an auction, the items they auctioned off were donated by local businesses. I reserved a dinner table for me and my family and donated four gift certificates. We enjoyed a nice dinner and then we watched our gift certificates get auctioned off.

This particular charity had a nice website, and they listed all the sponsors on it. They also had a program at the banquet that listed us as a sponsor next to our logo. When they sent out the emails to all their supporters, they thanked us for

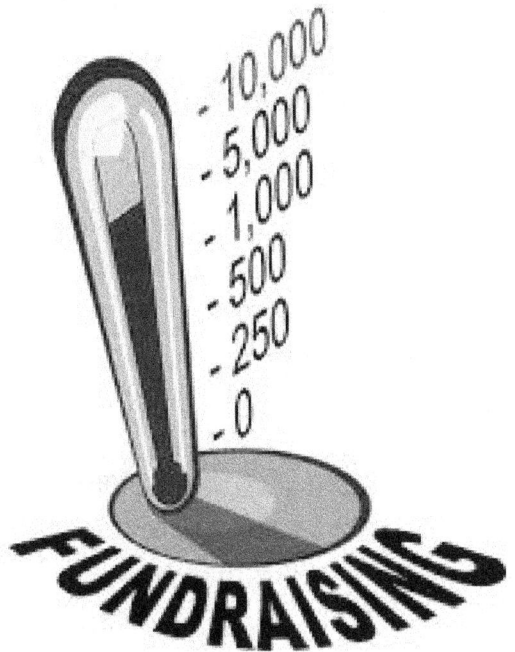

sponsoring the event in the body of the emails. It goes without mentioning that they showed plenty of gratitude during the event itself. We ended up gaining new customers from the exposure, and I have to admit I genuinely felt good about supporting their cause.

I know Susan G. Komen will allow you to use their name cosponsoring a special promotion at your company. To qualify, you must donate a percentage of your sales to their foundation as well as list them on your insurance for any promotional event. They may also require you to guarantee a minimum donation of $1,000 or so.

As I stated previously, Susan G. Komen holds many special events throughout the month of October. If you run a promotion with them, they will likely email a notice to their supporters and list your promotion on their online calendar as well as in their newsletter. They also have a massive following. Talk about great exposure.

Many of these charities will solicit you. I donated to four charities and I never actively went out seeking any of the four. Representatives from three of the charities came to our shopping complex to solicit to the businesses. An administrator of the fourth organization was actually a customer of ours. She mentioned the idea of cosponsoring an event during a visit to our business.

Bottom line is, you can gain some great exposure while performing a good deed. The exposure you gain through these promotions comes from the charities website, email blast, newsletter, programs, signage at these events, and promotional booths to name a few. Remember, the charity wants this event to be just as successful as you do.

TRUE STORY

The banquet I mentioned above held a unique raffle. A local jewelry store donated a half-carat diamond stone to the auction. Instead of auctioning off the diamond, they poured 200 glasses of apple cider into champagne flutes. Then they dropped a half-carat cubic zirconia into 199 of these flutes. The diamond was dropped into the last one. Obviously, nobody knew which glass the diamond was in except the staff selling the glasses of cider. Numbered tags from 1-200 were randomly placed around the stem of each flute.

My girlfriend, who was essentially my business partner at the time, actually bought me the glass that contained the diamond. I ended up giving her the diamond and planned on using it in an engagement ring for her. The engagement never happened, but I remain grateful for all her help building our business from the ground up. At any rate, it made for a great story around the office. Not to mention it was a nice little publicity stunt for the jewelry store.

HELPFUL HINTS

- Consider partnering up with a local business in the same shopping complex to co-sponsor an event together with a charity. This will work particularly well if the partnering business and the charity all have the same target audience as you. I partnered with Komen. My target audience was the same as the majority of their supporters.

- You can never go wrong attaching your business to a good cause.

NOTES: _____

_____

_____

_____

_____

_____

_____

Billboards

Before we get into advertising with billboards, I would like to go back to the two different marketing concepts I mentioned earlier in this book: share-of-market advertising and share-of-mind advertising. Share-of-market advertising attempts to gain immediate sales. Share-of-mind advertising attempts to gain future sales by implanting your brand in a person's mind. Billboards tend to fall heavily under the share-of-mind concept.

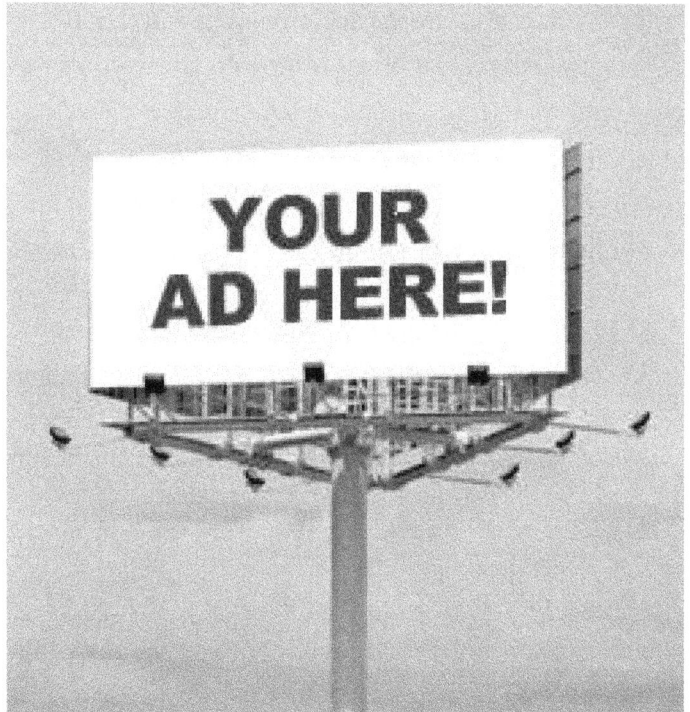

I am going to get right to the point: I do not think billboards are a good marketing tool for most small and micro-businesses. Usually, they will not immediately increase your sales. They are expensive, ineffective and mostly ignored.

They merely serve as reminders that you, as a business, are still in existence. As with everything in life, of course, there are exceptions. Remember the last time you were driving down the highway and saw the billboard that had a company's logo blown up and the words: Next Exit. In that instance, I would be willing to bet those billboards lead to more immediate sales, especially if the highway is in the middle of nowhere.

Oftentimes, the billboard companies won't just allow you to run a single billboard at a high traffic location. They prefer to set you up with a contract to run multiple boards at once. If they do allow you to run just one board, they may want you to sign a rotation contract where your board may be in a high traffic location one month and a low traffic location the month (or two) after that. However, sometimes they may allow you to run single billboards in ideal locations for a high premium or if they are trying to secure a contract with you.

I ran boards in Omaha, Nebraska in 2010 and 2011. The going rate was around $1700 per month on average. Another cost you have to consider is the graphics and design for the billboard. Many billboard companies can design your board for you, usually for a fee. The companies I have used printed the graphic onto a canvass that was 14' by 44'. They charged around $700 for each of these canvases. So if you wanted to advertise a holiday sale on the billboard, it would cost you a little over $700 plus the cost to design the graphics to be printed. Then your canvass is only good for a month or two out of the year.

For a billboard campaign to even have a chance of being truly effective you should rotate different advertisement designs. Otherwise you run a real risk of your billboard just blending in with the landscape. If people pass by the board on a regular basis, they are more likely to take notice of the board if it looks out of the ordinary. Once again you can count on paying thousands in design and printing fees to even have a chance at mounting an effective campaign.

Justin's Two-Cents:

"Billboardconnection.com is a resource you can use to find billboards and rates in your area, or even nationwide."

As a general rule, I would recommend the use of billboards to a few types of businesses. Billboards work very well for entertainment companies that put on concerts or large special events. As my previous example stated, they are also very useful to owners of restaurants, gas stations, and motels along highways that receive a lot of long distance travelers. Billboards can also be very useful if you are opening a new

location and want a lot of people to know about it especially if you tie in some kind of special grand opening promotion.

For most small businesses that do not have a lot of extra money laying around to throw on advertising I would not recommend billboard advertising. For most businesses it merely serves as a reminder to preoccupied motorists as they speed by. The amount of money you would have to devote to a billboard campaign to even have a chance of being effective could be spent so many different ways that could produce an instant return on your investment. When is the last time a billboard turned you into a paying customer?

TRUE STORY

I actually had a friend that worked for a billboard company. Of course she had been trying to talk me into using billboards. I am naturally skeptical of any advertising medium when I am told that I need to sign a one-year contract because it will take me at least half of that time to see any results. Once I told her this was out of the question, she tried to get me to try it for a month. This is after she told me I needed to run it for at least six months to be effective. (Another example of how these reps will tell you anything to get your money) At a bare minimum, I had to commit $2500 for a one month trial. I was a start-up and couldn't even imagine spending that kind of money on any one medium that was a big 'maybe'.

Instead, we ended up talking about digital billboards. These are slightly smaller than the regular 14' by 44' traditional boards. However, there was not a large up-front commitment required. I negotiated for them to do the design for the board for free. The company only had a couple of these boards and they were in prime locations. They wanted $500 per week for an advertisement that would stay up for ten seconds at a time. The digital billboard would actually rotate through twelve different businesses advertisements. Therefore, my ad would pop up once every two minutes and stay up for ten seconds at a time. I could also change the design of the ad during the week, if I needed to.

I ended up telling them my budget only allowed me to spend $350 and I would try the board if they would let me try it at that price for one week. They initially told me no, then called a couple weeks later and said they had an opening they couldn't fill and they would let me try it for $350 for a week. I ran it for a week and never got a single call on it. Remember, every customer that came through my door was asked how they heard about us. During this week, we even asked everyone who called our store how they had heard about us. Nobody ever mentioned the sign.

This billboard company had another digital billboard at a second prime location closer to our business and in a neighborhood that we marketed to. I ended up agreeing to try that sign for $400 for a week. We ended up with the same results as the first board: nothing. We actually had one guy call and set up an appointment and tell my receptionist that he had seen our billboard and called because he wanted to take advantage of the special offer we advertised on the board. However, he called a few days later and cancelled his appointment.

After this, I spoke to the many business owners I networked with and there was a consensus that none of them had really received enough leads from billboards to justify their cost. Most of those who had used them in the past had written them off as not worth the expense. Understand I am not basing this opinion solely off these two weeks I used in the example. By itself, this would not have been enough of a test to come to these conclusions.

As a side note, the billboards I used were actually very well designed. These were the same designs we had success with across other mediums. I had some assistance designing these ads from an advertising professional who was a friend of mine.

HELPFUL HINTS

- Try calling the local businesses you see advertising on the billboards in the area you would be interested advertising in. Talk to the owners of those businesses or the person in charge of marketing, and ask what kind of results they have received from the billboards. If they are not a direct competitor of yours you will probably get an honest answer out of them.

- Try digital billboards. They allow you to test different designs and campaigns without a long term commitment since there are no canvasses to purchase. The designs can usually be changed several times throughout the month or even throughout the week.

NOTES: _____

_____

_____

_____

_____

_____

_____

_____

_____

_____

_____

_____

_____

_____

_____

_____

_____

Signs

Businesses have been using promotional signs forever. They can be extremely affordable and effective. Signs come in all shapes, sizes and forms. With the price of commercial printing going down, signs are more affordable now than ever. This includes everything from 12" x 18" yard signs that lawn services and garage sales frequently use, to 4' x 8' wooden signs. There are so many different types of signs available these days.

Some signs can even be designed and printed using desktop publishing software, such as Microsoft Publisher. These programs can be great for printing promotional signs and posters that fit on a legal-size sheet of paper, or smaller. If you are going to need a large quantity of them, then the most cost-effective route may be to design one and save it into a digital file. Then you can either scan the original, or possibly send the digital format to a commercial printer for mass-production.

By networking with a nearby business owner, I obtained the phone number of a guy that printed signs out of his garage. These signs were surprisingly good quality, and very affordable. For example, he would print one-hundred, 12" x 18" white, corrugated-plastic yard signs for $169, as long as they were all the same design, and only had a message printed on one side. These came with stakes and were ready to go. This same guy printed a small adhesive sign for our front door that listed our business hours and contact information, for only $30. He even came out and applied it to our door.

Before you can plan your signs, you should lay out the exact action you want people to take once they see your sign. Then you need to make sure that desired action is going to be the likely result of someone viewing that sign. I recommend you have several unbiased people view your sign and tell you what is the first thing that comes to their mind. You should focus on random people who are also in your target audience.

You can also place these signs in the stores of your fusion marketing partners. After all, your prospects should be the same as their prospects and vice-versa. See about exchanging signs to place in one another's business. Signs act as a silent (and free) sales force.

Outdoor signs, including window banners, should be short and sweet. These signs are going to have fewer words than indoor signs. It is also generally a good idea to use one font for the entire sign. You will not have your prospects attention for very long. It would be best to not risk distracting them with different typefaces.

Outdoor signs need to stand out. If the sign is by itself, then it has a good chance of getting some attention. However, this is rarely the case. If it's a prime location for potential customer traffic, then chances are other businesses have signs there already. Just because there are other signs around, doesn't make it a lost cause. The goal now becomes to make your sign

really stand out from the crowd.

To get some ideas on how to make your sign unique, perform a Google Images search of "Effective Promotional Signs" to see some good designs. The main thing you want is contrast. You want your sign to really stand out from the crowd. If all the signs are in color, consider designing yours in black and white. If all the signs are rectangular, consider making yours a different shape.

A good practice is to take a picture of the area you are interested in placing your sign. Make sure you get all the competing signs in the frame. Then spend some time on your computer trying out different designs that clearly stand out from the crowd. Try pulling up the picture of the area on one side of the computer screen, and then pull up your designs on the other side. Compare and contrast.

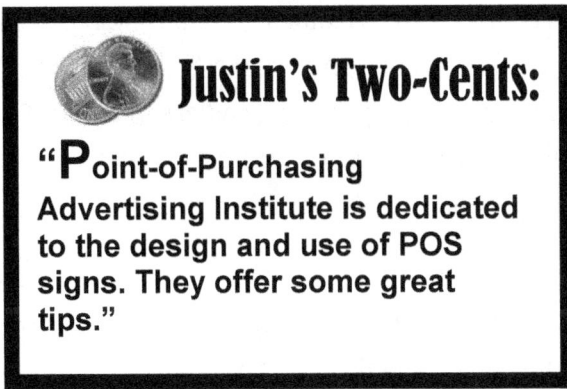

Justin's Two-Cents:

"**P**oint-of-Purchasing Advertising Institute is dedicated to the design and use of POS signs. They offer some great tips."

Whatever you do, don't stop at outdoor signs. Outdoor signs are meant to get someone into your store. Once you achieve this, it's not necessarily smooth sailing all the way to the bank from there. This is where indoor signs come into play. Unlike outdoor signs, indoor signs can utilize more wording. You do not have to compete with other companies here. These signs should be placed all around your store.

The most important indoor signs are point-of-sale (POS) signs. These signs are suppose to pick up where your ads and outdoor signs leave off. Don't limit yourself to just paper signs. Many businesses have digital monitors and displays in their stores. Consider even using video. I have seen several businesses use iPads or other tablets on specialized stands placed throughout their store.

A great practice to get ideas for designing POS signs is to simply go into other stores and see what works for them. Heck, go into all your competitors stores and see what they are doing. One thing you need to remember is that your signs, especially your POS signs, need to tie in with your other ads. These signs should remind people of your other ads they have seen.

TRUE STORY

At the beginning of this chapter I mentioned a guy that made yard signs, as well as the adhesive business hours signs for our front door. I mentioned that I found this guy by networking. Let me elaborate, I saw a sign in front of our shopping complex that I liked. This sign was advertising a neighboring business' 'Grand Opening' in our shopping complex. This sign was 4' x 8' and was made of a laminate-type material. I called the number on the sign and asked to speak to the manager. When she came on the line, I asked her where they had the sign made. This is how easily I obtained the phone number of this sign guy.

About a week after this phone call, their sign disappeared. I called back and asked why they had taken it down. They told me the complex manager allowed new businesses to place a sign like this up during their first month of being open. Then the sign had to be taken down after that. I contacted the landlord and was told they generally allow the signs for 4-6 weeks.

I contacted the sign guy and asked him to make me a similar sign. He made us a sign the same size and from the same material and installed it for me, all for $250! It was a great deal. The sign stayed up for over seven weeks. (By now you should know me well enough to know that when they told me 4-6 weeks I knew my sign would be up for AT LEAST 6 weeks.)

After about eight weeks, our sign was removed. At this point we had tracked over $2000 in sales attributable to this sign. Naturally, I started looking for a new place to put our sign. I noticed a pizza parlor in our complex had a similar sign that was located near one of the entrances to our complex. I called them and asked how they got permission to do this. They informed me the land was owned by a different management company and they had never asked permission, they just put the sign up and it had stayed there for over six months.

So, of course, I followed suit. I placed the sign up next to theirs, shortly before the winter. My thinking was that it would be hard for someone to remove when then ground was frozen, giving me at least four months of exposure. (The sign was held up by two 4" x 4" wooden posts that went about two and a half feet into the ground.) In the end, that sign stayed up until I sold my store. That $250 sign brought in over $4,000 in total revenue between the two locations.

This same sign guy made three window clings for me cheaper than anyone else could. These clings were about 42" tall x 30" wide. They had a UV protective coating over them to prevent fading since they had to be installed on the outside of our windows. He charged me $100 each to print and install them. (I already had the graphic design done) My other quotes were $150/each and $320/each. Both of the latter options would have required me to install them myself.

These sign guys are out there. The cost of these commercial printing machines has gone down considerably, allowing these one-man, garage operations to be possible. The quality is usually just as good too. Since these guys have no expenses such as labor, rent, and advertising (they usually rely on word of mouth), their prices tend to be much more affordable. I have met several other small-time guys like him since then. Network with other business owners until you find one that is as affordable and efficient as this guy was.

HELPFUL HINTS

- If you have a manufacturer or a parent company that supplies you with product, ask them to supply you with marketing materials as well. Oftentimes, these companies can (and will) give you free brochures, signs, banners, window clings, posters, and even display racks and stands, if you simply ask.

- By placing your signs in your fusion marketing partners businesses, you give the customer the impression that business is giving you an endorsement. This is great as they obviously have faith in that business, or they wouldn't be spending their hard-earned money there.

NOTES: _____

_____

_____

_____

_____

_____

_____

_____

_____

_____

_____

_____

_____

_____

_____

_____

_____

_____

_____

_____

_____

Referral Program

One of the most time-tested, best things a small business can do to promote itself is set up a referral program. This can be done in several ways. No matter which way you structure it, the underlying principle relies on the same thing: good, old-fashioned word of mouth publicity. Who better to refer someone than an existing happy customer?

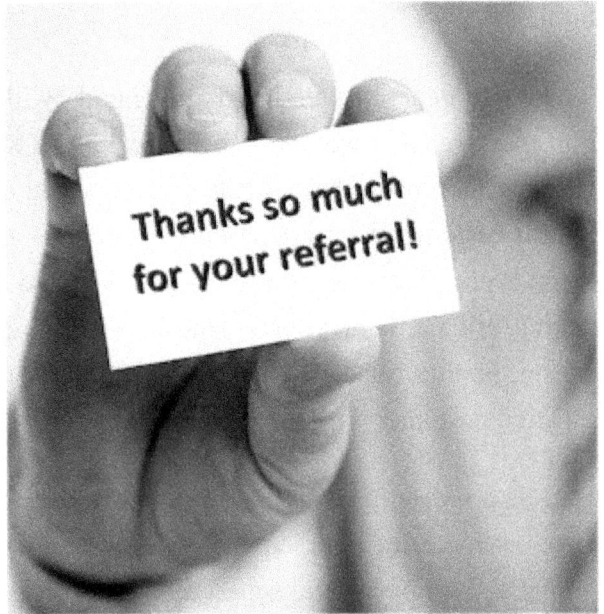

Setting up a referral program for your existing customers is one of the best ways to gain publicity. If someone has a good experience with your business they may mention it to their friends. Why not tilt the scales in your favor a bit? By offering some form of incentive to your customers, they are more likely to encourage their friends and family to visit your business rather than your competitors. Especially if they have had a good experience with your company.

Justin's Two-Cents:

"**N**obody is going to push your product for free. Don't be cheap. Offer your current customers something of value."

I have read some marketing books that say you should just ask your customers to give you referrals without offering anything in return. I disagree with this. We, as humans, love to be rewarded. By offering incentives to your current customers, it gives them some motivation to be a brand ambassador for your business.

People generally tend to have friends with similar interests as themselves. For example, if a woman likes to go to the spa and indulge in services there, chances are most of her friends do too. If you own a spa and this woman is your typical customer, then chances are her friends are in your target audience as well. With every customer you service, you have the chance to create a walking, talking billboard for your business. Adding an incentive to their next visit by asking them to refer their friends is an excellent way to capitalize on an already satisfied customer.

I also recommend setting up a referral program for other business-people to cross promote for your company. When I owned the cosmetic teeth whitening business, I set up several separate referral programs for business professionals in different professions including salon stylists, photographers and bridal boutique owners. I offered them a referral fee (A.K.A. kickback) for every paying customer they sent me. Many of these other professionals already have the trust of their customers and can be great advocates for your business. Think about a salon stylist. She has her client's ear for an hour or so (captive audience), and the client obviously trusts the stylist's judgment because she trusts her with her hair.

To monitor and track this system, I simply printed my own gift certificates using Microsoft Publisher. I inserted a unique code, assigned to each professional, in the bottom corner of each certificate. I then gave a stack of these certificates to each professional. The offer for the customer was usually $10-20 off of a service (which came out to about 10-20% off retail price). Then I usually gave the referring professional $10-20 per sale. I kept track of this in a simple spreadsheet.

Since we offered services with fairly high profit margins, I was able to offer larger discounts than some of you may be able to offer. It is the concept I am trying to teach you. You can scale this for whatever products or services you are in the business of selling. Every business has a customer acquisition cost. This is how much it costs you, in marketing dollars, to obtain a new customer. Be sure to keep this commission and discount structure in line with your current customer acquisition cost.

Keep in mind, both of the referral methods I mentioned cost me zero dollars to implement. The possibilities are endless. Be creative with structuring a referral program that is tailored to your business. Instead of asking your customers to send you referrals, go on the offensive. Ask them to provide names and contact info of three family members or friends who may also be interested in your products or services.

TRUE STORY

Teeth whitening is one of those things that needs a touch-up every so often. The referral system I set up for our current customers, offered a client a free touch-up session ($40 retail value) for every new client they referred to me. I had a few customers that had referred 4-5 people within a span of a couple months. At an averages sale of $149 each, you can see how valuable this can be. Many of our current customers just posted a picture of their teeth whitening results on Facebook and that was enough to send in referrals.

HELPFUL HINTS

- Consider partnering with other businesses to offer gift certificates to their stores instead of just your own. This can increase interest, while creating a good fusion marketing partnership. That business you partner with now owes you a favor.

- To increase the likelihood of your customer giving you names and contact info of referrals, tell them something along the lines of, "We can afford to keep our prices low by relying on our customers to give us referrals instead of spending a lot of money on advertising gimmicks". They will likely appreciate this and give you referrals.

Justin Bicket

Shopping Complex Discounts

In our shopping complex we had over fifty different shops, restaurants and offices. Some people may think this is bad because your business can get lost in the shuffle. This is not how I viewed it. As with everything in life, there are positives and negatives. The fact that we had such a large complex was great for two reasons.

First, the employees of the other businesses made up a large pool of potential customers. A good example of this is being a restaurant in the complex. All these people have to eat somewhere. This is an excellent opportunity to offer a discount to the employees of stores located in the complex. If you even have, say, thirty stores in your complex, and assume the average business has four employees on at any given time, that means there are 120 people that will be needing somewhere to spend their lunch break. This is an awesome opportunity to capture business without spending any marketing dollars.

When I ran one of these promotions, I simply printed out a basic flier for each business that explained who we were and what services we offered. I included the special promotion, which was a 20% discount, on the bottom of the flier. I also individualized the fliers for each different business by placing their name on the top. Then I dropped off a flier at every business: Simple as that! We probably clocked in a little over $1000 in revenue from this promotion in the first month.

The second way you can benefit from having a lot of neighboring businesses is by trying to feed off their traffic. Hopefully you have done well with selection of your business location and most of the neighboring businesses target the same type of customers as you. This allows you an opportunity to try to capture their attention while they are in the area. Hence the old business adage—"Location, location, location."

There are two different types of shoppers: destination shoppers and passive shoppers. Destination shoppers know what they want and drive to a particular business to buy it. A good example of a destination shopper is someone on their way to Wal-Mart to purchase a Playstation® 4. They are not there to browse through the different game consoles. They know exactly what they want and that is what they are there to buy.

Passive shoppers are those that do not know exactly what they want to buy. A good example of this is a woman going to the mall for a new outfit. She doesn't really know what she wants. She doesn't know whether it's a new skirt, or tank top & shorts, or maybe even a new swim suit. These shoppers only have a general idea of what they want to buy. The only thing they know for sure is that they plan on spending money on something.

The trick is not only getting the attention of these passive shoppers who are checking out the neighboring stores, but to also catch the eye of the destination shoppers as well. This is where you need to be creative. Use outdoor signs, window clings, signage in neighboring businesses, and any other creative ideas to capture the attention of both of these crowds. More businesses in your complex means more chances to obtain passive customers.

TRUE STORY

Our teeth whitening store's location was ideal. In the immediate vicinity of our store was a nail salon, medspa, massage parlor, weight loss center, bath & body boutique, tanning salon, and women's vintage clothing boutique. Needless to say, our location

> ## Justin's Two-Cents:
>
> "**I**s your complex busy on Saturdays? Is a neighboring business having a big sale soon? Consider having an employee canvass around your complex during times of increased traffic, handing out promotional fliers or coupons to your store."

could not have been any more ideal. It just so happens that the nail salon, that was located directly next door to us, was one of the most popular in the city. They had a constant stream of customers going through their door.

After seeing this, I realized I was missing out on a lot of potential leads that passed our store each and every day on their way to the nail salon, so I asked them if I could place a drawing box in their store. They said that would be fine. I also purchased a large sidewalk sign to place on the walk between our two stores. I designed the sign with a large graphic of a woman smiling, showing off her pearly whites, as well as sporting some freshly painted nails.

For the wording on this sign I chose to write: "Nice nails! How about a Smile to Match?" Then at the bottom, the sign said something about bringing in a receipt from the nail salon and receiving a 15% discount. I knew the clientele they had was the same we were shooting for. I could see many of the women sizing our business up from the outside while walking across the parking lot to the nail salon. This promotion did rather well.

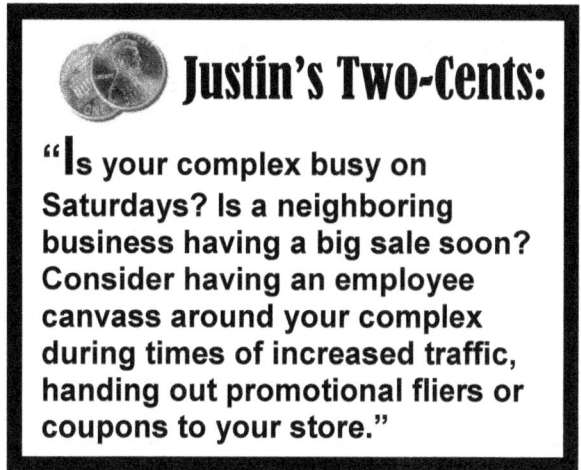

HELPFUL HINTS

- Be proactive and offer the employees of neighboring stores a 'plaza discount' to your store. This may spark the beginning of a mutually beneficial business relationship in the future. For example, they may be more inclined to allow you to place drawing boxes or a brochure rack in their store, in the future.

- Offer to place another business's brochures or fliers in your store. Once again, be proactive in pursuing fusion marketing partnerships.

NOTES: _____

_____

_____

_____

_____

_____

_____

_____

_____

_____

_____

_____

_____

_____

_____

_____

_____

_____

Miscellaneous Marketing Mediums

There are many mediums that were not covered in the previous chapters of this book. This section is dedicated to analyzing some of these mediums that were not quite elaborate enough for an entire chapter to be devoted to them. This is not to imply that these are bad mediums, it's just that most of them can be broken down in a couple paragraphs or so. Just as with the previous chapters, some of these mediums are excellent ideas, others are a waste of time and money.

Live TV Segments

Most cities and metro areas have regional TV shows that are comparable to local versions of 'Good Morning America'. Many of these shows allow businesses to 'sponsor' the show in exchange for airtime. I have done this a few times and found it to be very effective. One show I was featured on charged about $550 for a 6-7 minute live segment. These shows usually allow you to submit the questions you would like the host to ask you. This way your segment is virtually scripted.

These shows are not going to be a sure-fire hit for every business. First, you must evaluate the shows audience. Does it primarily reach the same prospects

you are after? If it does, then your next step is to determine if your product or service is something that would benefit from live TV coverage. For example, I advertised teeth whitening on one of these shows. It was the perfect medium for this because we performed a teeth whitening procedure on an actual customer, live on the air. This was important for us because the audience knew the results couldn't be doctored or photo-shopped in any way.

We talked the producer into allowing us to split up our segment. They did not want to do this, but I told them that if they didn't allow us to split it, then it was a deal-breaker for us. (From my experience, the producers do not like to do this.) The first six minutes of the segment consisted of me starting the procedure on set, while being interviewed. During the first commercial break, we took all our equipment and our customer off set, and finished the procedure there. Then, during the very last segment, the hosts called our customer back up on stage and compared before and after shots the cameraman had zoomed in and taken live on the set. We wanted to demonstrate two things: the ease and simplicity of the procedure, and the results.

If you need to educate the public about your business or product, this can be a great medium to look into. These shows can also be a good idea if your product or service is something that needs to be demonstrated. The fact that the coverage is live allows the audience to lower their guard. These shows are the TV equivalent of an editorial piece. Most of the audience believes that you are featured because the station is endorsing your company, not that you simply paid to be featured.

Movie Theaters

Have you ever went to a movie theater early to get a good seat, and seen the ads that run across the

screen before the previews start? Some comedy clubs also have similar projector screens that display ads before their shows. These are avenues of advertising that most businesses never think about. One of the pluses to this type of advertising is that not many other businesses do this. Another plus is the fact that you have a captive audience, with a humongous screen displaying your ad, ensuring that the audience has no choice but to take notice of your ad.

This does not necessarily mean this type of advertising is a good idea. It all comes down to the price point. If you are going to purchase this type of advertising, it had better be cheap. For one, there are usually not that many people that arrive to the theater this early. I would venture to guess that more people arrive late rather than early.

Secondly, you have no control over targeting your ad to a specific demographic other than maybe selecting the movie you want your ad to run before. This is actually closer to the shotgun approach of marketing that has been discussed, and frowned upon, earlier in this book. However, I would recommend at least exploring this avenue if you can pin your demographic to a particular film.

For example, I once created a promotion for a guy who owned a comic book store. This guy knew his comic books and superheroes, but knew nothing of the marketing side of his business. When the newest Ironman movie was released for a midnight screening, we ran these ads before the movie. For these high-demand midnight premieres, people show up hours before the movie to wait in line to ensure they get a good seat. Needless to say they are excited, which is the perfect frame of mind to be advertised to. So we knew there would be plenty of excited prospects in the theater.

While everyone was in the theater, we canvassed the parking lot and placed two fliers under the windshield wiper of every car. Meanwhile, the ad inside the theater made reference to the special promotion that was advertised on the fliers. The comic book store had a really great turnout from this promotion. This is also an example of how two separate mediums can be used cohesively to form an effective marketing campaign. The ad inside placed the thought of this comic book store in the minds of people before the movie who, apparently, are fans of comic book heroes. After the movie was over, the fliers on the cars reminded them of the same promotion. Not to mention, these people were already in an excited state of mind during the time both of these marketing messages were put in front of them.

Canvassing

The previous story had an excellent example of canvassing in it. Canvassing can be a great way to promote your business, inexpensively. Canvassing requires more of a time commitment, than a financial one. Even if you send teams out to do your canvassing, you still have to map out their routes. One way that canvassing can be used effectively is, just like the example above, having a team place fliers on the windshields of cars.

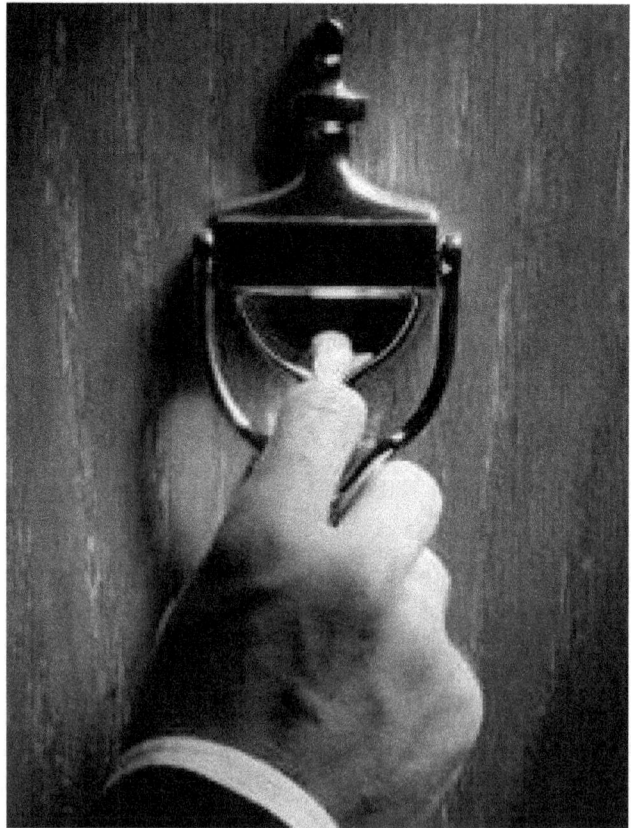

This may sound like a shotgun approach, but if you are smart, you can target certain audiences. This requires creativity. The type of creativity that was used in the comic book store example. There are not many places where you can find a bunch of avid comic book fans congregated outside of a comic book trade show or convention.

Find events that are happening in the neighborhoods you advertise in. I do not recommend sending canvassing teams out without any direction. Placing fliers under every windshield wiper you see can turn many people off. You need to send your team to areas or events that will likely be full of people interested in your products or services.

Another way canvassing can be successful is by placing doorknob hangers on doors of the neighborhoods you are trying to reach. You should be able to recruit anybody from friends and family members, to high school and college students to be part of your canvassing team. Make sure your canvassing effort does not cost you as much as, or more than, a direct mail campaign would. Canvassers usually work fairly inexpensively. On average, canvassers should be able to hit 70-80 houses, or at least twice that many vehicles, in an hour. You need to employ trustworthy canvassers and ensure they actually place the fliers or hangers. I have seen instances where the canvassers throw away the fliers and go spend the day at the mall, instead.

School Sports Programs & Newspapers

If your target audience consists of high school or college students, consider advertising in their student newspaper. These papers are generally not viewed by anyone outside of that particular student body, and the ads are usually designed by students learning graphic design (unless you design your own ad). However, these ads are priced with this in mind. They are usually relatively inexpensive. I have run these ads for as low as $20-30 each.

If your target audience consists of the parents of students, then consider advertising in school sports programs. These programs are usually all read by the parents of the student athletes, cheerleaders, band members, etc... Since their kids are featured in them, they pay close attention to them, and several parents even keep them. Not to mention that most high school, and even some college, sports events are not very exciting in the first place. Many of these parents may not admit it, but they will gladly entertain any distraction. This includes reading ads of local businesses that offer a special discount to the parents of students of that particular school. Once again, these ads are usually very inexpensive. However, they may require you to advertise for an entire season for each sport though.

Door Magnets & Other Promotional Products

Many of you have probably seen the magnetic signs that people place on their car doors, advertising their business. These magnets are great for three reasons. First, they turn your car into a moving billboard. Everywhere you drive, you are promoting your business. Secondly, they can offer a tax benefit since everywhere you drive can be considered an advertising expense. (Disclaimer: Please talk to your tax professional before writing this expense off. I am not attempting to offer any tax advice and I am not a tax professional. Ughhh, we live in such

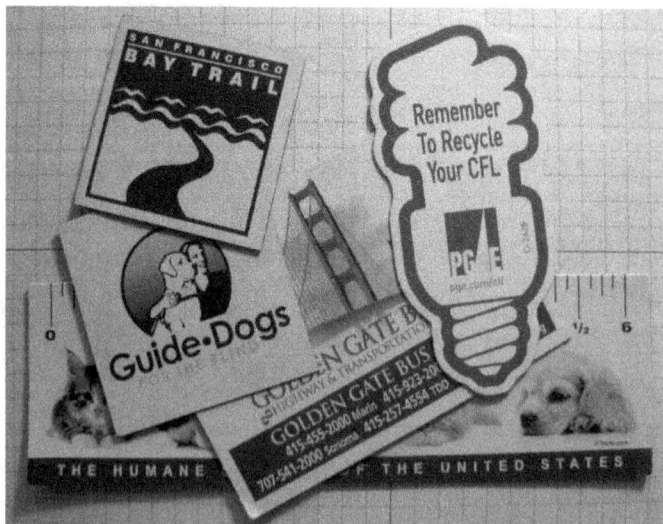

a litigious society...) Lastly, they are removable.

There are other ways you can use your vehicle as a promotional tool, however most of these other ways include a permanent or semi-permanent decal being affixed to your vehicle. This may be fine if your vehicle is a dedicated company vehicle. But if your vehicle doubles as you personal vehicle as well, this can be a bit tacky. This is the main reason I opt for the door magnet signs. They are usually about 12" x 18" but can be slightly larger or smaller, and can be easily removed. They are relatively inexpensive as well.

There are so many different promotional products out there that can be customized with your company's logo and/or contact info. You can visit sites such as AliBaba.com to find products from anywhere in the world. I remember I almost bought a case of new MP3 players I had found from a vendor on their site. These MP3 players greatly (and probably illegally) resembled Apple's iPod Shuffle. At this time, these were one of Apple's big sellers, before the iPod touch. These knockoff MP3 players were relatively inexpensive, and would have had my logo and contact info on them, all for under $20 each. I thought it would make for a great promotional item. However, I did not want to deal with the legalities involved with importing Copyright or Trademark-infringed goods.

AliBaba.com serves as a worldwide, virtual marketplace where companies from all different countries sell almost anything you can think of. There are many different promotional items that can be purchased inexpensively in bulk through the vendors on this site. I have found many companies that will personalize virtually anything. You can also find many foreign, mass-printing companies that specialize in signs, brochures, and business cards, on this site. Many of these items are great ideas for handouts trade shows.

Backs of Receipts

Have you ever gone to the grocery store and seen a bunch of coupons printed on the back of your receipt? This is another advertising gimmick that is popular.

Notice the word I used was popular, not effective. I also used the word gimmick as opposed to medium. This pretty much sums up my thoughts on this useless tactic.

Receipts are annoying pieces of paper that clutter up men's pockets and women's purses. If we save a receipt, it is usually because we may need it to either return something, or use it for tax purposes. Either way, we are not likely to flip it over and cut out a 1" x 2" coupon printed on the back of it. As a consumer, I had taken notice of these receipts long before this rep ever wandered into my store. I have even tried keeping these receipts, thinking I was going to redeem one of these coupons one day. Then, I get tired of seeing a bunch of crumpled up receipts in my cup holder and center console of my car, and start feeling like a hoarder. Needless to say, they always get thrown away. I have yet to actually redeem one. Nor have I found anyone who has.

Now, I am sure there are some extreme couponers who actually use them, but I am sure these people are few and far between. The vast majority of people simply throw them away. My mom is one of the biggest coupon-clippers I know, and I have yet to see her use these. When a rep actually came out to my store and tried to sell me on this idea, I started to collect these receipts from the various stores I shopped at. I did my own research. I called the companies that advertised on these receipts and inquired about their success. The overwhelming response mirrored what is written

above. Apparently, they have a high turnover and a low re-sign rate for their advertisers.

Balloons!

No, I am not suggesting you hire a clown to do balloon animals. (However, if your target demographic is kids or even parents, this can be a creative idea.) I am referring to the use of balloons, similar to what you may have seen outside of a car dealership during a big sale. I am talking about large, colorful, heavy-duty, helium-filled, outdoor balloons. These balloons are often as large as six feet in diameter. They can usually be found at dedicated balloon stores or in shops specializing in party supplies.

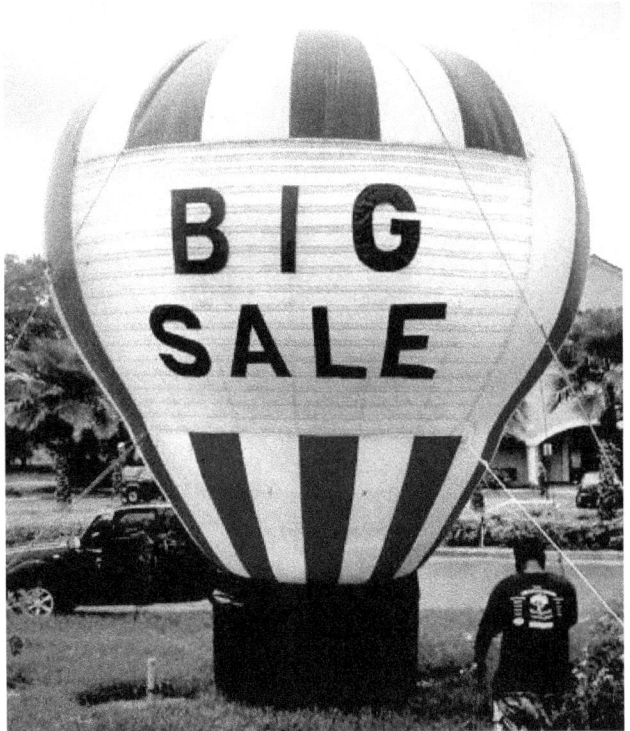

Our shopping complex would often hold special events during which it experienced times of high foot traffic. It was during these events that I would use these balloons to pique the curiosity of passers-by. I also used them a lot when we had our 4' x 8' sign up in the beginning. I actually found this to be fairly successful. I would hang smaller balloons from our sign. Then I would go onto the roof of our store and hang much larger balloons of the same color as the smaller ones. I would usually choose balloons that had the word 'SALE' written in very large letters on them. Instead of using regular a string to anchor the balloons, I would use a string of colorful pennants.

Afterthoughts

I hope this book has given you the insight I have intended. Like I said before, this book will not spell out the exact answer for every marketing question. However, I am confident that if you have read all the way to this point, you understand the principles contained in this book. If you understand the underlying principles, then you should be able to figure out these answers on your own. Hopefully you have learned something that will actually help you. If you have not, then it is because you are either too close-minded, or you are more savvy in marketing than I am and you already know all of these things. (Which is entirely possible) If this is the case, I urge you to pass this information on to another small business owner.

The examples I used were simply to show you how the principles explained in each chapter have actually worked in the real world. Many people teach concepts that sound really good on paper, but sometimes we have a hard time figuring out how they would play out in the real world. I made sure that I did not fill this book with 'fluff'. I have read a lot of business books, and one thing I have realized is they are full of filler material, or fluff. This is material that is really nonessential, and is used to make a book thicker. Authors think that if a book is 300-400 pages their readers will think there must be something of value contained in it. I do not subscribe to this philosophy.

I would like to thank you for taking the time to read my words. This is the part where I wish you the best of luck in all your endeavors. I do wish this for you, but as for my real advice...make your own luck.

References

Business Review Sites:

- MerchantCircle.com

- Yelp.com

- Google.com

- Yahoo.com

- RipOffReport.com

- PissedConsumer.com

- CitySearch.com

- AngiesList.com

- TripAdvisor.com

- UrbanSpoon. com

- OpenTable.com

- Insider Pages

Affiliate Marketing Sites:

- ClickBank.com

- CJ.com

- PayDotCom.com

- LinkShare.com

- Amazon Affiliate Program

- Affiliatematch.com

- Refer-it.com

Website Design & Development:

- landl.com

- Elance.com

- Guru.com

- RentACoder.com

- ScriptLance.com

- HighPowerSites.com

- ThinkBigSites.com

- LivePerson.com

Dailey Deal Sites:

- Groupon.com

- LivingSocial.com

- OfficeArrow.com

- GroupPrice.com

- MarketSharing.com

- BizyDeal.com

- MarketBlitzDeals.com

Other Useful Sites:

- TaskRabbit.com - Hire out a job, small project or task to a freelance virtual assistant.

- TopSEOs.com-- Rankings and ratings for businesses that specialize in SEO, direct-mail and email campaigns.

- WebsiteOptimization.com-- See how fast your web pages load.

- AnyBrowser.com-- See how your web pages will look on all browsers.

- SpamHaus.com-- Site allows you to check the credibility and reputation of internet hosting sites. (Some get blacklisted for allowing illegal email campaigns. If you choose one of these sites, unknowingly, your site will be blacklisted as well.)

- KeywordDensity.com-- Check your web pages keyword density. (A density between 2-5% is ideal)

- BackLinkWatch.com-- Get info on which sites post links to your competitor's website.

- MarketingSherpa.com-- Get data that applies to your industry

- EasyWebAutomation-- Manages all affiliate programs and has a great virtual shopping cart.

- RSStoJavaScript.com-- Tool to add RSS feeds to your website.

- SubmitYourArticles.com-- Small fee-based service that distributes your articles to a number of reputable sites.

- Afingo.com-- Alibaba-type site for the fashion industry.

- TSNN.com-- online directory of over 17,500 trade shows and conferences.

- Click2mail.com-- have postcards, fliers and greeting cards sent directly to your customer's door.

- ComScore.com-- Market Research Company that will evaluate your e-commerce site.

Internet Keyword/Phrase Services:

- FreeKeywords.wordtracker.com- track what people are searching for on search engines (daily info).

- Adwords.google.com/select/keywordtoolexternal- measures keyword searches by month.

- KeywordDiscovery.com- information on which keyword searches are most popular

Professional Freelance Services:

(Article writing, graphic design, programming, web development, etc...)

- Elance.com

- Guru.com

- ScriptLance.com

- RentACoder.com

About the Author

Justin Bicket did not take the road well-traveled in becoming a successful entrepreneur. A troubled youth battling ADHD and legal troubles as a teenager, he found his calling in one of the most unexpected places…a jail cell with a copy of Robert Kiyosaki's *Rich Dad, Poor Dad.* This was all the inspiration he needed. He overcame his adversity and later attended the University of Nebraska on scholarship.

He is now a loving father of two daughters, Karra and Kyra. He has been involved with many start-ups ranging from entertainment companies, to retail stores, and even some consulting work. He is also involved in a half dozen or so internet-based start-ups. He also spends time mentoring struggling small businesses and start-ups in the area of marketing.

www.ingramcontent.com/pod-product-compliance
Lightning Source LLC
Chambersburg PA
CBHW051409200326
41520CB00023B/7170